OBJECTIVE MENTAL MEASUREMENT

OBJECTIVE
MENTAL
MEASUREMENT

Individual and Program Evaluation Using the Rasch Model

Robert M. Hashway

PRAEGER PUBLISHERS
Praeger Special Studies

New York   •   London   •   Sydney   •   Toronto

Library of Congress Cataloging in Publication Data

Hashway, Robert M
  Objective mental measurement.

  Bibliography: p.
  Includes index.
  1. Intelligence tests. 2. Rasch, Georg, 1901–
I. Title.
BF431.H348   153.9'3   78-19739
ISBN 0-03-046476-5

Published and Distributed by the
Praeger Publishers Division
(ISBN Prefix 0-275)
of Greenwood Press, Inc.,
Westport, Connecticut

PRAEGER PUBLISHERS,

PRAEGER SPECIAL STUDIES

383 Madison Avenue, New York, N.Y. 10017, U.S.A.

Published in the United States of America in 1978
by Praeger Publishers,
A Division of Holt, Rinehart and Winston, CBS, Inc.

89   038   987654321

Printed in the United States of America

To Peter Airasian, George F. Madaus, and Ronald L. Nuttall

PREFACE

The science of mental measurement has experienced rapid growth in this century. Its role has grown from attempting to address the basic issues encompassing the measurement of intelligence to offering assessment instruments in a variety of cognitive and affective domains. Much of this growth has been stimulated by societal needs. As western culture achieved greater technological sophistication, the fields of education and psychology also developed technologically, resulting in the development and refinement of sophisticated theories of learning and other human processes.

Measurement played a large role in the metamorphosis of the behavioral sciences. Psychologists and educators embarked upon a refinement of their knowledge of human processes. In this quest they adopted the observation and measurement scenario which worked well in the physical and biological sciences. Instruments were developed in an attempt to assess the human attributes which were incorporated in the rapidly emerging theories (confirmatory studies). The instruments were also used to explore possible relationships that might have existed and were yet to be explained or predicted by the existing theories (exploratory studies).

The growth of Government and foundation funding in the area of human service delivery systems added a new component to the emerging disciplines: the competition for limited resources. Previous to the growth of external funding sources, much of the research which was performed in applied settings concerned the benefits and attributes of particular programs. Little research was done comparing different programs with similar intents relative to a set of common criteria. Program evaluation and applied research emerged as a result of the competition for the limited resources creating additional demands for measurements. Instruments were required which addressed the objectives associated with the growing number of human service agencies.

The growing human science discipline and human service industry has not only resulted in a need for more instruments of various types, but also for a more sophisticated technology designed to construct those instruments. The technological growth of the discipline of human attribute measurement has not paralleled the growth in other areas. Although certain multivariate techniques such as factor analysis and clustering procedures have found some applicability in the process of instrument construction, the basic item-difficulty and item-total score correlation scenario remains the predominate item selection technique. In fact, factor analysis and clustering techniques are strongly dependent upon item-difficulty and interitem correlations.

Procedures for program and treatment evaluation continue to be entrenched in statistical models which are based upon agricultural and biological measurement models. Unfortunately, the nature of behavioral measurement is such that the precision of 'hard' science data is almost never realized. Therefore, the statistical treatment of evaluation data is based upon assumptions concerning measurement precision which are unrealistic expectations. To the present time no attempt has been made to integrate the nature and structure of human measurement models into statistical inference procedures.

A major quantal jump in the theory of mental measurements has recently been proposed by Rasch (1966). The Rasch model is a theory of measurement with is fundamentally different from what has become the traditional paradigm. Tests constructed to conform to the Rasch model are said to exhibit properties which Wright (1967) called 'Objective Mental Measurement.' Of major interest to human science professionals should be the property that if equivalent Rasch tests are administered to a particular individual the scores obtained from the tests do not seem to be very different (Hashway 1977). In fact, observed differences between two Rasch test scores obtained from the same individual seem to be of much lower magnitude than would be expected from the intervention of random error (Hashway 1977).

The literature concerning the Rasch model currently exists in numerous technical journals and widely dispersed technical reports. This book is, in part, an attempt to summarize much of that material and present it in one central reference. New material is also presented.

Presently, the research reported in the literature has focused upon the properties of the Rasch model. Little attention has been paid to the application of tests composed of items that conform to the Rasch model. This volume contains models and procedures with which Rasch tests can be used for individual assessment and program evaluation. Procedures by which the test scores can be used to assist in making educational and/or program decisions at the individual level are discussed. Statistical procedures for using Rasch test scores for program and treatment evaluation are also presented. These statistical techniques are based on a fundamental model of behavioral measurement. It is felt that results obtained from the application of the procedures are more representative of behavioral phenomena than the results obtained from the application of procedures based on a different level of measurement specificity.

The second chapter and much of the preliminary thinking for the evaluation models were developed while the author was a doctoral candidate in the Division of Educational Research, Measurement and Evaluation at Boston College. That work was conducted as the author was completing a doctoral dissertation under the direction of Dr. George F. Madaus. The author wishes to acknowledge the valuable comments and suggestions rendered by Dr. Madaus.

In addition, Drs. Peter Airasian and Ronald Nuttall contributed greatly to the dissertation of which this volume is an extension and elaboration. This volume's focus on basic presentation of theory and application is due in great measure to the influence of Dr. Airasian on the author's professional attitudes. Much of the prerequisite theory was generated as a result of casual conversations with Dr. Ronald L. Nuttall. The author wishes to acknowledge and extend his gratitude to these people for their assistance and suggestions. The author also wishes to thank Drs. Frank B. Corriea, James Bierden, and John Nazarian for the training in advanced analysis and mathematical statistics afforded him while a graduate student in the Mathematics Department at Rhode Island College. Although many people have made comments, suggestions and various contributions to this book, the responsibility for any errors or misstatements rests with the author.

CONTENTS

LIST OF TABLES

LIST OF FIGURES

1

INTRODUCTION

Tests of ability or attainment have been used for a number of purposes. One purpose for the standardized test is to initially screen students in an attempt to determine those students who satisfy particular criteria unique to particular programs. Another purpose is to track pupil attainment over time in order to determine pupil progress. An additional use of standarized tests is to assess the effectiveness of particular programs. The latter use of standardized tests is often intended to answer one of two questions. One question program evaluations attempt to answer is whether or not a particular program is achieving the objectives for which it was intended. A second issue is whether or not one particular program or group of programs are more or less successful than other programs designed to achieve the same objectives.

Recently, the use of standardized tests has been strongly criticized (see reviews in Block and Dworkin 1976). Some of the issues that have been raised concerning the use of standardized tests will be reviewed in the second chapter of this volume.

A court action with important implications for programs for the handicapped has been pending in federal district court in San Francisco since 1971. That court action is a class action suit, Larry P. v. Riles. The lawyers for six minority elementary school students have alleged that their clients were wrongfully placed in classes for the educable mentally retarded on the basis of their clients' scores on standardized intelligence tests. The Wechsler, Stanford-Binet, and Leiter tests were specifically mentioned in the suit. These tests are, perhaps, the most commonly used tests of general intelligence. The attorneys for the plaintiffs have attempted to present evidence that the tests are culturally biased in the sense that they reflect "middle-class" experiences exclusive of the experiences of students with different backgrounds. Regardless of the outcome of the San Francisco court action, the testimony presented is like to have some effect on testing and evaluation programs.

In addition to the issues outlined above, some researchers have criticized the use of standardized tests for the purposes of program evaluation. Some have argued that standardized tests tend to assess the abilities of students within a global content domain that is too broad to reflect subtle program differences (Airasian and Madaus 1976; Carver 1975; Rakow, Airasian, and Madaus 1976). Others have addressed the issue on psychometric grounds (Cobean, Airasian, and Rakow 1975; Harvey 1975; Hashway 1976; Rakow, Airasian, and Madaus 1975). Standardized test items are selected in a purposeful fashion (Ahmann and Glock 1967; Ebel 1954; Guilford 1954; Gulleksen 1950; Lord and Novick 1974; Nunnally 1967). The purpose of the selection procedure is to discriminate maximally between individuals (Ebel 1954; Guilford 1954; Henryssen 1971; Lord and Novick 1974). Robert Hashway (1976) has demonstrated on mathematical grounds that these that maximally discriminate between individuals are totally ineffective for detecting treatment or program differences.

The use of standardized tests, therefore, presents somewhat of a dilemma. The use of these tests as indicators of individual attainment or ability presents many problems. In addition, the tests do not seem to be effective for detecting program differences. Most program administrators and practitioners will agree that some uniform procedure for assessing attainment and program effectiveness is necessary. The conflict between the need for uniform measurements and issues surrounding most of the existing measurement instruments presents a dilemma for the administrator of testing and evaluation programs.

The twentieth century has seen the development of many tests of ability or attainment. The tests of ability were designed to assess how much of a particular construct a subject possessed and to predict the degree of success a person would experience in the performance of a task. The tests of attainment were developed to assess the degree of success a subject experienced in mastering a particular subject matter area after a period of instruction and relative to a calibration group. Both tests of ability and attainment were intended to differentiate between individuals according to the amount of ability the individuals possessed or the degree of subject matter attainment the subjects possessed (Matarazzo 1972; Sundberg and Tyler 1962; Terman 1916, 1919; Terkes 1921; Spearman 1927).

Refinements in the procedures used to construct these tests have been made (Lord 1952; Thurstone and Thurstone 1941; Carroll 1950; Wherry and Gaylord 1944; Lord and Novick 1974). However, the main assumption and the basic model underlying the test construction technique have remained unchanged. That assumption is that the subjects are normally distributed over the ability dimension (Matarazzo 1972; Lord and Novick 1974). The number of subjects who possess a particular ability level correspond to that number that would be expected from a normal probability density function (Harris 1966; Freund 1962). Item selection techniques, which are traditionally used to construct typical tests, are designed to ensure a normal distribution of test scores (Lord and Novick 1974; Guilford 1954).

B. D. Wright (1967) has criticized traditionally constructed tests on two psychometric grounds: the score received by a particular individual is a function of the items used to construct the test, and the score obtained by a particular individual is a function of the group used to standardize the test. As a corollary, Wright (1967) also argues that tests should produce scores that exhibit two characteristics: two tests purporting to assess the same ability or attainment domain result in the same scores for the same person, and a test score should not be a function of the group used to calibrate the items included in the test.

Consider two traditional tests containing the same number of items and constructed from a group of items that are associated with the same content domain. Assume that one test is composed of very difficult items and the other test is composed of less difficult items. Tese scores obtained by a particular individual will depend upon which test was administered to that individual. The same individual will obtain a test score from the second (easier) test that will be numerically larger than the result that would have been obtained if the difficult test was administered. The two tests would not be "item-free." In addition, a traditional test designed to assess achievement in basic algebra is not applicable to high school students if the test was calibrated using a sample of elementary school students. Traditionally, if a test was not calibrated using a sample that is not similar to the population for which the test was intended to be used, little confidence can be placed in the resulting test scores. Traditional tests are not "sample-free."

G. Rasch (1966) has presented an item selection technique that is intended to produce tests with characteristics corresponding to those described by Wright (1967). The Rasch procedure purports to result in tests that are both sample-free and item-free. That is, the scores results from Rasch's tests purportedly are not a function of the items used to construct the tests or the samples used to calibrate the instruments. The technique is similar to Thurstone scaling in that both items and individuals are scaled (Edwards 1957).

Tests designed to comply with the assumptions of the Rasch model possess two very interesting and useful properties. These properties have been discussed in great detail by Wright (1967; Forbes 1976; Forster 1976; Mead et al. 1974; Tinsley 1971; Whitely and Dawis 1974, 1976; Wright and Douglas 1974; Wright and Panchapakesan 1969). Tests constructed using the Rasch model are said to be both item-free and person-free. The tests are item-free in the sense that two Rasch tests that contain items assessing the same content domain yield two scores for the same individual and these scores are not appreciably different (Hashway 1977). It has been demonstrated that the scores obtained for a particular person from two equivalent Rasch tests differ by an amount appreciably less than expected from a purely random error of measurement function (Hashway 1977).

Items that compose a Rasch test are said to be person-free in the sense that the value of the psychometric parameters associated with those items are not dependent upon the population of subjects used to estimate those parameters (Boldt 1972; Brink 1972; Forbes 1976; Forster 1976; Hashway 1977; Ingebo 1976; Mead et al. 1974; Tinsley 1971; Whitely and Dawis 1974; Willmott and Fowles 1974; Wright 1975; Wright and Mead 1975). Because the scoring formula for Rasch tests is functionally dependent upon the item parameters, the scoring formula and the Rasch scores are person-free. It appears that tests constructed with the Rasch model are viable alternatives to the traditional standardized tests. Rasch tests do not possess the "undesirable" properties frequently associated with traditionally constructed standardized tests.

Unfortunately, a serious problem exists that tends to prevent the widespread use of tests developed with the Rasch model. This problem does not concern the Rasch tests themselves, but rather the interpretability of the scores at the level of the practitioner and program specialist.

The Rasch model belongs to a general class of test construction models called logistic latent trait models (Lord and Novick 1974). The model assumes that items or subjects are assignable to particular locations on a unidimensional latent trait dimension. In addition, the Rasch model provides a particular mathematical statement relating the probability with which a particular subject will experience success relative to a particular item in terms of the location of the subject and item on the latent trait dimension. The details concerning the particular functional relationship associated with the Rasch model will be described in Chapter 2. The underlying latent trait dimension, however, is assumed to be a line of infinite extent.

Tests constructed using latent trait models result in scores that may attain any value whatsoever (from negative infinity to positive infinity). For example, a particular subject may obtain a Rasch score of 4.195, another subject may obtain a Rasch score of -3.215, and a third subject may obtain a Rasch score of exactly 0. It should be clear that these scores are not easily interpretable as are traditional test results, such as percentile ranks or the number of items responded to correctly.

The purpose of this volume is to describe procedures by which teachers, administrators, and program evaluators will obtain a better understanding of Rasch tests and their application. Procedures by which Rasch measurements can be interpreted and utilized for program evaluation will also be described.

The remainder of this volume is organized into three major chapters. Chapter 2 describes the Rash and traditional test construction models and critically reviews the research conducted to date concerning the Rasch model. Chapter 3 presents a model of Rasch test scores in terms of true scores and measurement error. In addition, Chapter 3 describes procedures by which the Rasch test scores for a particular individual obtained using the same or equivalent tests on two distinct occasions or between test scores obtained by two individuals can be compared. Chapter 3 also contains a description of procedures by which Rasch test scores can be converted to more familiar scales (such as T-scores), and the implications of those transformations. Chapter 4 extends the measurement model developed in Chapter 3 to the problems associated with program evaluation. The evaluation and experimental models presented in Chapter 4 are the two-group comparison problem, the pretest-posttest design with treatment and control groups, the repeated measurement design, and the multilevel factorial design. The technical details presented in Chapters 3 and 4 are supplemented by numerical examples intended to exemplify the application and amplify the theory.

2

A CRITICAL REVIEW
OF RESEARCH CONCERNING
RASCH AND TRADITIONAL MODELS

This chapter reviews the current literature concerning the Rasch model, and is divided into five sections. The first section is a discussion of the traditional psychometric techniques for test construction. The second section delineates some of the shortcomings associated with tests constructed using traditional psychometric techniques which tests constructed with the Rasch model supposedly do not possess. The third section describes the major theoretical differences between the Rasch and traditional techniques. The fourth section describes the procedures used to select items that fit the Rasch model. The fifth section critiques the state of current research concerning the Rasch model.

THE TRADITIONAL ITEM SELECTION TECHNIQUE

The traditional psychometric item selection procedures are not dependent upon the content domain or construct for which a test is designed and are used to construct tests of both attainment or ability. As the same item selection procedure is applied in building tests of ability or attainment, no effort will be made to define the constructs of ability or attainment at this point.

Fundamentally there is a single model common to both the Rasch and traditional psychometric item selection procedures. That is, there exists some attribute intrinsic to an individual and shared by all individuals that functions as a constraint on the probability that a person will respond in the correct fashion to an item or group of items. The attribute most often is not directly observable and is inferred from the responses of subjects to the items. This attribute has been called a latent trait (Lord and Novick 1974; Hambleton and Cook 1976). There may be different latent trait dimensions that underlie the responses to different tests. For example, the attribute dimensions underlying the responses of subjects to vocabulary and calculus tests are most likely quite different. It is also possible that the same latent dimension may be underlying the responses to two different but similar tests. For instance, two tests of arithmetic proficiency may be related to the same latent trait dimension.

A latent trait continuum or dimension is assumed to exist. The probability that a subject will respond correctly to an item is assumed to be a function of the subject's position on this dimension. A test is a functional mapping from the categorical set of individuals onto the latent trait dimension. The mapping function is subject to the constraint that the probability of responding correctly to an item is a monotonic increasing function of positions on the latent trait dimension (Nunnally 1967; Guilford 1954). The constraint implies that the higher a subject's position on the latent dimension the greater the probability that the subject will respond correctly to the item.

It has been pointed out that the traditional psychometric paradigm is subjected to an additional constraint (Harvey 1975; Lord and Novick 1974). This constraint is that the items are selected in such a way as to maximize the dispersion of test scores. The total test score should maximally discriminate between individuals (Harvey 1975; Henryssen 1971) and the score distribution should be "spread out as much as possible" (Lord and Novick 1974).

Establishing the Item Pool

The process of constructing a test starts with a list of specifications or content areas to be included in the test. An achievement test purporting to measure achievement in a limited area may have a very limited list of specifications. A test purporting to measure a broad range of abilities, or some general ability, may have a very large list of specifications.

Items that appear upon inspection to be related to the specifications are included in the test. This process ensures that the test will have face validity (Nunnally 1967). The set of items generated forms an initial item pool or a preliminary version of the test. The preliminary version is administered to a group of subjects. The group subjects are selected so that they are similar to the group for whom the final version of the test is intended. The responses of the pretest sample of subjects to each of the items in the preliminary version of the test constitute the initial item pool data bank. The initial data are subjected to traditional psychometric screening. As a result of that screening, decisions are made as to which items are to be included in the final version of the test and which items are not.

The traditional item selection procedures have been described in detail in the literature (Gulliksen 1950; Guilford 1954; Nunnally 1967; Lord and Novick 1974). The traditional psychometric screening procedure is outlined below.

The Traditional Item Screening

Traditionally, three major areas of concern in screening items are homogeneity, internal consistency, and the maximal dispersion of test scores. A group of items are homogeneous if the subjects who respond correctly to an item tend to respond correctly to all other items in the group and receive high total test scores, and if the subjects who respond incorrectly to an item tend also to respond incorrectly to all other items in the group and receive low total test scores. A group of items are internally consistent if the probability of successfully responding to an item is a monotonic function of a subject's position on some latent trait dimension. If subjects with similar positions on some latent trait dimension respond in similar ways to all items, the group of items are said to be internally consistent. If a test is composed of items selected so that the total score variance is larger than it might have been given any other set of items the test is said to have maximal total score dispersion (Lord and Novick 1974).

An index of item homogeneity is the item discrimination index. The discrimination index of an item is, most often, the correlation coefficient between the obtained item scores (correct/incorrect) and the total test score. In the case where an external criterion is available, the discrimination index can be defined as the correlation of the item score and the external criterion score. As the discrimination indices of items increase, the resulting test becomes more homogeneous (Ahmann and Glock 1967). The more homogeneous a test the greater the likelihood that the items and the total score are assessing one, rather than more than one, latent trait dimension. If an item pool contains items that are not homogeneous, the discrimination indices of the items can be used to determine those items that, when combined, form a more homogeneous subset of items (Ahmann and Glock 1967).

There are various indicators of the degree to which a test is internally consistent. These indicators are internal consistency reliability estimates. The indices or estimates vary from a low of zero to a maximum of one. The higher the internal consistency reliability estimate the greater the internal consistency of the test.

In index of internal consistency reliability is the Kuder-Richardson Formula 20 (KR-20) (Nunnally 1967). This index is calculated using the number of items composing the test, the mean total test score, and the total score variance. The KR-20 reliability index is probably the most easily calculated and the least accurate of the reliability estimates. The KR-20 reliability index is not directly related to the patterns that may exist between item scores. The KR-20 internal consistency reliability estimate is perhaps the most global estimate of internal consistency.

A less global index of internal consistency, in the sense that it is more sensitive to variations between items, is the split-half reliability index (Gulliksen 1950). The items are divided into two tests. The split-half reliability is the correlation coefficient between the total test scores obtained from each half. There is a problem associated with using the split-half reliability index, however. Different indices can be obtained depending upon how the items that composed the halves were selected. The correlation coefficient between two halves constructed by randomly assigning items to halves may be a function of the randomization procedure.

An index of internal consistency reliability that is not as global as KR-20 and does not possess the problems of the split-half index is the Kuder-Richardson Formula 21 (KR-21). For binary items, KR-21 is equivalent to Cronbach's alpha coefficient (Gulliksen 1950; Nunnally 1967; Guilford 1954). This coefficient is equivalent to the mean of the reliability estimates obtained over all possible split-halves (Lord and Novick 1974; Guilford 1954; Nunnally 1967).

Although each of the internal consistency reliability indices mentioned above results in somewhat different numbers for the same set of items, the results obtained are usually similar. A high internal consistency estimate obtained using one method will usually imply that a high internal consistency estimate will be obtained using another method.

The reliability of a test is closely related to the correlations of the item scores with each other, as well as with the total score. The more homogeneous a test the greater its internal consistency and the larger the internal consistency reliability estimates. The correlation between item and total scores has been defined as item discrimination. The higher the discrimination index of each of the items in a test the greater the homogeneity and the larger the internal consistency. R. L. Ebel (1954) contends that items with discrimination indices less than .20 should not be included in a test. Items with discrimination indices above .20 should be considered for inclusion. Items with discrimination indices above .40 are considered to be very good items in the sense that they discriminate between adjacent positions on the latent trait dimension (Ebel 1954; Ahmann and Glock 1967).

Another statistic commonly used to screen items is item difficulty. The difficulty of an item is the proportion of subjects who respond correctly to the item. It is easily demonstrated that a total score distribution of a test will have maximal dispersion if all the items have a difficulty level of about .7071.

The total score will be spread out as much as possible if approximately 71 percent of the subjects respond correctly to each item. If items are selected that have a difficulty level other than .71, the distribution of total scores will not be as spread out as much as it would be if the items had a difficulty of .71.

Tests that contain items whose difficulty levels are all exactly .50 have a maximum KR-20 internal consistency reliability index. A general rule of thumb has been presented that is a compromise between maximum reliability and maximum spread of the observed score distribution. Ebel (1954) states that items should be considered for inclusion in a test if their difficulty indices are between .40 and .70. This general selection criterion should result in a test with a moderately high reliability and a reasonably well dispersed observed-score distribution.

In summary, items selected for inclusion in a test using traditional psychometric techniques should have certain properties. These properties tend to ensure that the resultant test is homogeneous and internally consistent, as well as possesses a reasonably well-dispersed total score distribution. The point-biserial correlation between the scores obtained by the subjects in the calibration sample in response to an item with the total score should be greater than .20. The proportion of subjects in the calibration who respond correctly to an item considered for selection should be between .40 and .70.

PROBLEMS RELATED TO TESTS COMPOSED
OF TRADITIONALLY SCREENED ITEMS

This section discusses some of the problems that have been purported to exist with tests composed of items that have been screened traditionally. The particular problems discussed are those which the Rasch model purportedly does not possess.

All tests, regardless of item selection procedure, assume that there exists some latent dimension that underlies the probability of responding correctly to an item or group of items. A test score maps subjects onto a scale considered to be equivalent to the latent dimension. A person is assumed to occupy one and only one position of the dimension at any one point in time. Therefore, two tests constructed from an item pool calibrated on the same set of individuals and considered to map subjects onto the same dimension should result in the same or similar scores for the same individual. Wright (1967) has considered this property to be fundamental to what he calls "objective mental measurement."

It is well known that tests constructed by traditional means and purporting to be related to the same latent dimension are usually highly correlated (Matarazzo 1972). The fact that two tests are highly correlated implies only that the tests order subjects in similar ways. There is a difference between similar orderings of subjects and similar scores for the same subjects. Similar ordering of subjects means that the position of a particular subject relative to the other subjects in a group is not a function of the test used to obtain the subject's score. Similar scores for the same subject mean that the scores derived for the same subject from two or more tests are not significantly different. Tests constructed using traditional psychometric techniques and representing the same content domain may rank order subjects in the same way. In most cases two tests, constructed traditionally, do not result in similar scores for the same subject. The results obtained from traditionally constructed tests do not correspond to what Wright (1967) has called the item-free property. That is, an individual score on a latent trait dimension is independent of the particular set of items used to measure that position.

The generalizability and applicability of a traditionally constructed test to a particular group of individuals are related to the degree to which the particular group corresponds to the group used to calibrate the traditional test. A test whose items were screened using an upper-middle-class sample of subjects may not be applicable to lower-class subjects. A test designed to assess achievement in advanced calculus whose items were screened using a sample of high school seniors is not applicable to college physics majors. If a traditionally constructed test is administered to a group that does not correspond to the characteristics of the calibration group, the amount of confidence that can be placed on the score is zero. The scores obtained from tests constructed traditionally are not sample-free.

The fact that the score obtained from a traditionally constructed test is a function of the items used to construct the test, and that the meaning that can be associated with a score on a test is a function of the group used to calibrate the test, has led Wright (1967) to term traditional test scores "rubber yardsticks."

The model proposed by Rasch (1966) is intended to overcome the rubber yardstick problem. Wright (1967) contends that Rasch tests conform to what he calls an "objective mental measurement." Rasch tests are purported to be both item-free and sample-free (Wright 1967). The score assigned to an individual is not a function of the items selected from the same calibrated item pool to construct the instruments that assign those scores. Also, the same raw score has the same interpretation regardless of the group used to calibrate the item used to construct the instruments from which the score was derived.

The scores obtained from Rasch tests can be expressed in terms of ratio scales. The zero of the scale is operationally defined as the position on the latent trait dimension that corresponds to a zero probability of responding successfully to an item. The Rasch scores obtained by two individuals can be directly compared. Two tests obtained from the same Rasch test can be directly compared. Although the ratio scale property is useful in some applications, most research has been done using logarithmic Rasch scores. The logarithmic Rasch score is the natural logarithm (base e) of the ratio level Rasch score. The logarithmic score is an interval rather than a ratio level measurement. The point of zero probability of success is located at negative infinity on the latent trait dimension. All of the discussion of the Rasch scores from this point will assume that logarithmic measurement scales are being used.

In summary, tests constructed by the Rasch procedure are said to possess two properties not associated with traditionally constructed tests: Rasch scores are said to be item-free in the sense that two tests constructed from the same calibrated item pool using the Rasch model result in equivalent scores for the same individual; and the same raw score has the same interpretation regardless of the group used to calibrate the items composing the tests by which the scores are obtained, and hence the Rasch test is sample-free.

The procedures for selecting traditional items and the problems associated with traditionally constructed tests that are not supposedly associated with Rasch tests have been discussed in the preceding sections. The remainder of this chapter is devoted to three major areas: the theoretical differences between traditional and Rasch models, the details concerning the selection of Rasch items, and research conducted to date.

THEORETICAL DIFFERENCES BETWEEN RASCH AND TRADITIONAL TECHNIQUES

The Rasch and traditional psychometric models make one common assumption, that the probability of responding correctly to an item is some function of a subject's position on a latent trait dimension. The latent trait is considered to be representative of an attribute that is common to all subjects. Although the underlying dimension is considered to be common to all people, each person may occupy one and only one position on the dimension at any one time. A particular person cannot be given more than one score by the same test at a particular administration.

Both models assume that the latent dimension is unidimensional (Thurstone and Thurstone 1941; Wright 1967). The unidimensionality assumption implies that the latent trait corresponds to a single attribut dimension. If the probability of responding correctly to a particular item or group of items is largely a function of one and only one attribute dimension, the corresponding latent trait dimension is said to be unidimensional.

Traditionally, the unidimensionality assumption is closely associated with the factor analysis literature. The presence of one common factor explaining a large amount of the observed covariation between items has been considered an indicator of unidimensionality (Thurstone and Thurstone 1941). The psychometric difficulties with this procedure have been described in the literature (Thurstone and Thurstone 1941; Carroll 1950; Wherry and Gaylord 1944). These psychometric difficulties concern the nature of the correlation coefficients used to calculate the factors, and the fact that item level data do not represent a continuous level of measurement.

There is a question concerning the use of the factor model that has not been addressed. The mathematics involved in generating the common factors starts with a correlation matrix and results in what is known as eigenvectors of that matrix (Rummel 1970). A common factor is one of the eigenvectors. There is no ensurance resulting from the application of any mathematical procedure that the results are similar to any substantively meaningful concept. Furthermore, it has been pointed out that the structure of the factors obtained from the application of the mathematics varies depending upon the composition of the population used to generate the correlation matrix (Thurstone 1938). The resulting structure of a factor analysis is dependent upon the subjects used to generate the item level scores, which is, in turn, used to generate the correlation matrix upon which the mathematical procedure depends. Therefore, there is no reason to believe that the factor model is any better indication of unidimensionality than any other algorithm.

The unidimensionality assumption of the Rasch model seems to be more global and somewhat more general. R. J. Mead (1974) points out that an item that does not fit the Rasch model may not be unidimensional in the sense that a single latent trait is not sufficient to explain the observed item response patterns. A strict interpretation of the unidimensionality assumption would imply that a test of arithmetic skills would require separate scales for items related to addition, subtraction, multiplication, etc. This strict interpretation has been empirically tested by F. W. Forbes and G. S. Ingebo (1975).

They found that it was possible to obtain Rasch item calibrations from a composite item pool without first performing a subtest breakdown. This can be interpreted in two ways: the Rasch model may be sufficiently robust with respect to violations of the unidimensionality assumption, or the unidimensionality requirement is sufficiently broad as to encompass a global trait, such as arithmetic skills.

The Rasch and traditional psychometric scaling procedures are based upon the assumption that the position of a subject on a latent trait dimension will govern the probability of a subject responding correctly to an item. The major difference between the two techniques concerns how each assumes position on the latent trait dimension and how this is related to the probability of responding correctly to an item. The major difference between the two techniques is in the functional equation that defines the action of the constraint.

The Rasch and traditional psychometric techniques assume that certain relationships exist between the subject's position on the latent trait dimension and the probability that the subject will respond correctly to an item. The relations are defined in terms of a mathematical function. The function defines the probability that a person with a particular latent trait score will respond correctly to an item (Lord and Novick 1974; Hambleton and Cook 1976). This function is called the item's characteristic function (Kifer, Mattson, and Carlid 1975; Hambleton and Cook 1976). The graph of the function is called the item's characteristic curve (Kifer, Mattson, and Carlid 1975; Hambleton and Cook 1976).

The traditional psychometric technique assumes that the characteristic function is the same for all items. This characteristic function is the cumulative distribution function for a Gaussian variable (Lord and Novick 1974; Guilford 1954). If P(x) represents the probability that a person located at position x on the latent trait continuum will respond correctly to an item, this probability can be expressed as follows:

$$P(x) = (2\pi)^{-\frac{1}{2}} \int_{-\infty}^{x} e^{-\frac{1}{2}t^2} dt \tag{2.1}$$

where t is the dummy variable of integration.

The integral on the right of Equation 2.1 is not expressible in terms of an elementary function (Harris 1966). However, the value of the integral can be approximated using numerical techniques. Using the approximations to Equation 2.1, the graph of P(x) vs. x can be drawn (Hashway 1974). That graph is the characteristic curve assumed to exist for an item selected using the traditional paradigm. The graph is shown in Figure 2.1.

FIGURE 2.1   Characteristic Curve of a Traditional Psychometric Item

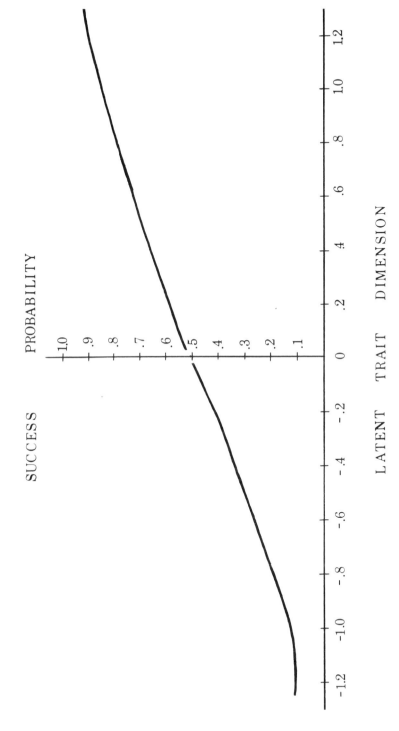

Source: Constructed by the author.

15

Figure 2.1 shows that the traditional paradigm assumes that the probability of responding correctly to an item is a monotonic increasing function of the subject's position. The more positive a subject's position the greater the probability of responding correctly to the item. A higher probability of success indicates that a more positive position on the latent trait dimension is required.

Characteristic Function Differences

Rasch (1966) has raised some major questions concerning the traditional model. The traditional model assumes that the characteristic function corresponding to each item is the same for all items (see Figure 2.1). This implies that a person with a particular latent trait score has the same probability of responding correctly to all items. It is not inconceivable that, for a particular individual, some items may be either more or less difficult than others. It follows that some items may in general for all people be more or less difficult than others. Assuming that some items can be more or less difficult than others, it follows that the probability of responding correctly to a set of items is a function of both the subject's position on the latent trait dimension and the item under consideration. The Rasch model assumes the existence of a characteristic function that is functionally dependent upon both the position of a subject on the latent trait dimension and the position of the particular item under study on the same latent dimension as the subject's position was determined.

Characteristic Functions of Rasch Items

In the Rasch model, each item is assumed to occupy a position on the latent trait dimension. The more positive the position of the item the more difficult the item is considered to be in terms of the number of subjects who respond correctly to the item. Each item is considered to have a characteristic curve of its own. The characteristic curve corresponding to one item need not be the same as the characteristic curve corresponding to another item. Unlike the traditional technique, which requires all items to have the same characteristic curve, the Rasch model assumes that each item has its own characteristic function. That is, the Rasch model takes into account differences that may exist between items (Rasch 1966; Wright and Panchapakesan 1969).

The characteristic function corresponding to a particular item is defined in terms of the position of the item on the latent trait dimension and the position of the subject on the same dimension. If item i is located at position a_i on the latent trait dimension, the probability of responding correctly to the item, given that a subject is located at z, is expressed as a function of the distance between the subject and the item, $a_i - z$. The probability that a subject located at position z on the latent continuum responds correctly to an item located at a_i on the same continuum is expressed by $P(a_i, z)$.

$$P(a_i, z) = [1 + e^{a_i - z}]^{-1} \tag{2.2}$$

The characteristic functions corresponding to three items located at three different positions along the latent trait dimension are shown in Figure 2.2.

Equation 2.2 and the curves described in Figure 2.2 indicate that the probability of responding correctly to an item is a monotonic increasing function of the difference between the position of the subject and that of the item, $a_i - z$. Subjects who occupy positions lower than that of the item tend to have a lower probability of responding correctly to the item than subjects who occupy positions greater than that of the item.

Rasch Item Difficulty

The position of an item on the latent trait dimension is called the item's difficulty. The greater an item's difficulty the more difficult the item appears to be. An item's difficulty is defined as the point on the continuum where it is expected that a subject would have a probability of .50 of responding correctly to the item. For example, the three items whose characteristic curves are shown in Figure 2.2 are located at positions of .20, 1.0, and 2.0 on the latent dimensions. Subjects who occupy a position of .20 (z = .20) on the latent dimension can expect a 50 percent probability of responding correctly to item 1. Subjects located at a position of 1.0 (z = 1.0) on the latent dimension can expect a probability of .50 of responding correctly to item 2.

The difficulty index used with Rasch items is not the same as the difficulty index with traditionally screened items. Traditionally, item difficulty is the proportion of subjects responding correctly to the item. The Rasch difficulty index is the position on the continuum where the probability of responding correctly to the item is .50.

FIGURE 2.2   Item Characteristic Curves for Three Rasch Items

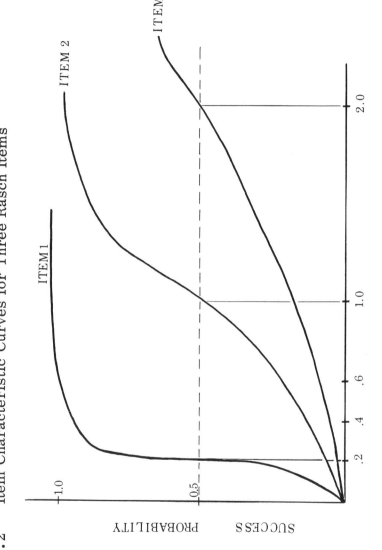

Source: Constructed by the author.

18

Rasch Item Discrimination

Another parameter associated with Rasch items is what is called an item's discrimination index. Item discrimination can be thought of as an index of how well the item discriminates between ability levels (Kifer, Mattson, and Carlid 1975). The indices of item difficulty and discrimination are described in the latent trait literature. There, definitions can be found in most standard texts, such as that by F. M. Lord and M. R. Novick (1974).

Consider the item characteristic curves described in Figure 2.2. A horizontal line drawn at the probability of success level of .50 intersects each of these curves at exactly one point on each curve. The discrimination indices for each of the items is the slope of the characteristic curve at the point where the probability of success is .50. The discrimination indices corresponding to the three items whose characteristic curves are depicted in Figure 2.2 are 99.0 for item 1, 1.0 for item 2, and .50 for item 3. A high discrimination index (much greater than 1.0) indicates that a subject whose position on the latent dimension is greater than that of the item will most probably respond correctly to the item and a subject whose position is less than that of the item's position will respond incorrectly. A low item discrimination (much less than 1.0) indicates that the probability of successfully responding to the item is uniform and that the item does not discriminate well between ability levels.

The discrimination index used with Rasch-selected items is not the same as the index by the same name used with items selected traditionally. The traditional item total score correlation ranges between -1.0 and +1.0. The discrimination index used with the general latent trait model can take on the value of any positive or negative real number. The Rasch model assumes that all items have the same discrimination index and that this index is 1.0 for all items. The equality of item discrimination is a consideration in selecting items for inclusion in a Rasch test (Wright 1975; Wright and Mead 1975; Mead et al. 1974; Wright and Douglas 1974; Wright and Panchapakesan 1969). This topic will be discussed in greater detail in the next section.

As outlined above, the Rasch model has two basic properties: score invariance and item difficulty invariance. By the score invariance property it is meant that given a set of items that satisfy the Rasch assumptions and that two or more tests are constructed from these items, the scores obtained by the same individual from each of the tests will be statistically equivalent (Wright and Panchapakesan 1969). The item difficulty invariance property means that if the same set of items is administered to two different groups and the data obtained from each group are used separately to obtain Rasch item difficulty indices, the indices obtained using each of the groups will be statistically equivalent.

The major theoretical differences between the Rasch and traditional psychometric paradigms have been pointed out. These differences concerned different assumptions about the functional item characteristic curve; and the fact that the Rasch model assumes that both items and subjects occupy positions on the latent continuum, whereas the traditional model assumes that only subjects occupy positions on the continuum. Some of the properties of the Rasch model have also been described, including score invariance and item difficulty invariance. The details concerning the Rasch item selection procedure will now be described.

CONSTRUCTING TESTS USING THE RASCH MODEL

The theoretical differences between the Rasch and traditional psychometric models have been outlined. The traditional psychometric technique for screening items has also been described. The traditional technique results in a set of items that satisfy the normal ogive characteristic curve model. The procedure described in this section is used to select items that satisfy the Rasch assumptions.

The parameters used to select items can be obtained by applying the computer program CALFIT to item level data (Wright and Mead 1975). This program obtains maximum likelihood estimates of the item parameters (item difficulty and discrimination) and person parameters (Rasch test scores). Details concerning the estimation procedures and the structure of the subroutines are described by Wright and Panchapakesan (1969), as well as by Wright and Mead (1975). The mathematical details are also described by E. W. Kifer, I. Mattson, and M. Carlid (1975). The reader interested in those details or the preparation of CALFIT command control cards is referred to these sources.

CALFIT is a computer program written in FORTRAN IV. The program uses a classical numerical procedure called the Newton-Rapson method to estimate item and score group parameters. A mathematical function called the log likelihood function (Wright and Panchapakesan 1969; Wright and Mead 1975) is computed. The particular log likelihood function describes the relationship between the observed proportions in the item x score group matrix and the Rasch parameters. The objective of the program is to obtain parameter estimates that extrimise the log likelihood function. The iterative procedure continues until the differences between parameter estimates obtained from two consecutive iterations are negligible. When the likelihood function is extrimised, the cell probabilities calculated from the parameter estimates represent the best fit to the observed probabilities, given the constraints of the Rasch model.

Fit Mean Square

The first parameter of interest when screening items using the Rasch procedure is called the fit mean square. This statistic is a measure of the degree to which the item's characteristic function, given the estimated difficulty and discrimination parameters, fits the postulated logistic curve. The fit mean square is a measure of the degree to which the observed item characteristic function conforms to the model represented by Equation 2.2. The larger the fit mean square obtained for a particular item the more the item's characteristic curve departs from the Rasch logistic function. The smaller the fit mean square obtained for a particular item the greater the correspondence between the observed characteristic function and the function postulated by the Rasch model. The fit mean square is asymptotically distributed as an F-statistic with N - 1 and an infinite number of degrees of freedom for the numerator and denominator, respectively (where N is the number of score groups used for calibration).

For example, when six score groups are used for calibration, the critical value of the F-ratio at the .05 significance level is 2.2. A value of the fit mean square greater than 2.2 implies a lack of fit between the item's characteristic function and that assumed by the Rasch model. A value of the fit mean square less than 2.2 implies that the item tends to fit the Rasch model (Wright and Mead 1975). Thus, if the fit mean square is greater than 2.2, the item should be rejected. If the fit mean square is less than 2.2, the item should be given further consideration.

Rasch Discrimination Criterion

The second criterion for item selection is the Rasch discrimination parameter. The Rasch model assumes that all items have the same logistic discrimination parameter. The assumed value of the discrimination parameter is 1.0. An estimate of the discrimination index for each item is obtained using CALFIT. This estimate is derived from item data. Because the number of items are finite, there is a degree of error associated with this estimate. This error is called the standard error of the item discrimination estimate. If the estimated item discrimination plus or minus three standard errors is within the range of .80 to 1.20, the item is said to have satisfied the item discrimination criterion. If the estimated item discrimination plus or minus three standard errors is not within the range of .80 to 1.20, the item is said not to have satisfied the discrimination criterion (Kifer, Mattson, and Carlid 1975).

Items that satisfy both the fit mean square and the item discrimination criteria are considered to be suitable for inclusion in Rasch tests. Items that do not satisfy both criteria are not to be included.

Establishing a Rasch Score Formula

Once the items that fit the Rasch model have been selected, a method of transforming a subject's responses to these items into Rasch scores must be devised. A result of using the computer program CALFIT with the initial set of items is a table that describes the relation between raw total scores (the number of items answered correctly) and the Rasch score. This table is based upon the entire initial item pool. The table resulting from the initial screening is not based on only the items that fit the model but all of the items used. The revised scoring formula is obtained by using the program a second time, considering only those items that fit the model as a result of the initial screening.

The Rasch model assumes that the latent trait dimension upon which the subjects are mapped is continuous. The position of a subject is determined by responses to a finite number of items. The measurement of the position of a subject on some latent dimension is analogous to measuring the length of an object 4.5 in. long with a ruler marked only in inches. It can be determined that the object is greater than 4 but less than 5 inches long. Any attempt at a precise measurement of the length of the object will be the result of some estimation process. Because the Rasch procedure assigns scores to subjects and the subjects are assumed to be located on a continuum (using a finite ruler), the question becomes, What is the error of the measurement estimate?

The Rasch scoring formula obtained using CALFIT results in a mapping from the number of correct responses to the subject's position on the latent trait dimension. An index of the accuracy of the estimate of the subject's position is also obtained. This index of accuracy is called the standard error of the ability estimate.

The greater the number of items located about the subject's estimated position on the latent dimension the more accurate the estimate of the subject's position and the smaller the standard error of the ability estimate corresponding to that position. This corresponds to measuring the length of a block 4.5 in. long with a ruler marked in 1/8-in. units as opposed to a ruler marked in 1-in. units. The accuracy of the estimated length with the ruler marked in 1/8-in.

units will be greater than the accuracy obtained with a ruler marked in 1-in. units.

The Rasch model assumes that a subject's score is not estimable if none or all of the items are answered correctly. It is common practice to obtain a score for a subject who has not responded correctly to any of the items by subtracting one standard error from the score corresponding to a total score of one item answered correctly. The score associated with a perfect score on a test composed of k items is found by adding one standard error of the ability estimate to the Rasch score corresponding to k - 1 items answered correctly (Kifer, Mattson, and Carlid 1975).

The mapping of the number of correct responses to Rasch scores can be displayed graphically. A typical form of such a graph is shown in Figure 2.3. The number of correct responses form the horizontal axis and the Rasch scale scores form the vertical axis. To find the Rasch score that corresponds to a particular raw score: (1) find the raw score on the horizontal, or raw score, axis; (2) from the point on the raw score axis, draw a vertical line to the graph of the mapping function; (3) from the point where the vertical line intersects the mapping function, draw a horizontal line to the Rasch score axis. The point where the horizontal line crosses the Rasch score axis is the Rasch scale score corresponding to the initial raw score. For example, the Rasch score corresponding to a raw score of 9, given the mapping function in Figure 2.3, is +.75.

Once a Rasch test has been constructed and a scoring formula established, the raw score for each subject can be translated into many of the popular derived test score reporting paradigms (for example, stanines, percentile ranks, z-scores) using the same procedures that apply to traditional test scores. The transformed scores may be more easily interpreted by the less mathematically sophisticated user. However, all but linear transformations (such as transformations to z-scores or T-scores) will change the interval nature of the scale and may result in a noninterval level of measurement. The major advantage of the Rasch procedure lies with its item and sample invariance properties.

Reliability of Rasch Tests

The graph in Figure 2.3 is typical of the type of contour that results from the application of the Rasch procedure described above. This mapping function is nonlinear. The raw score versus Rasch score profile is not a straight line. This nonlinear relation presents some difficulties for the assessment of Rasch test reliability. The indices used to assess the reliability of a traditional test assume that

FIGURE 2.3   A Typical Rasch Raw Score Mapping Function

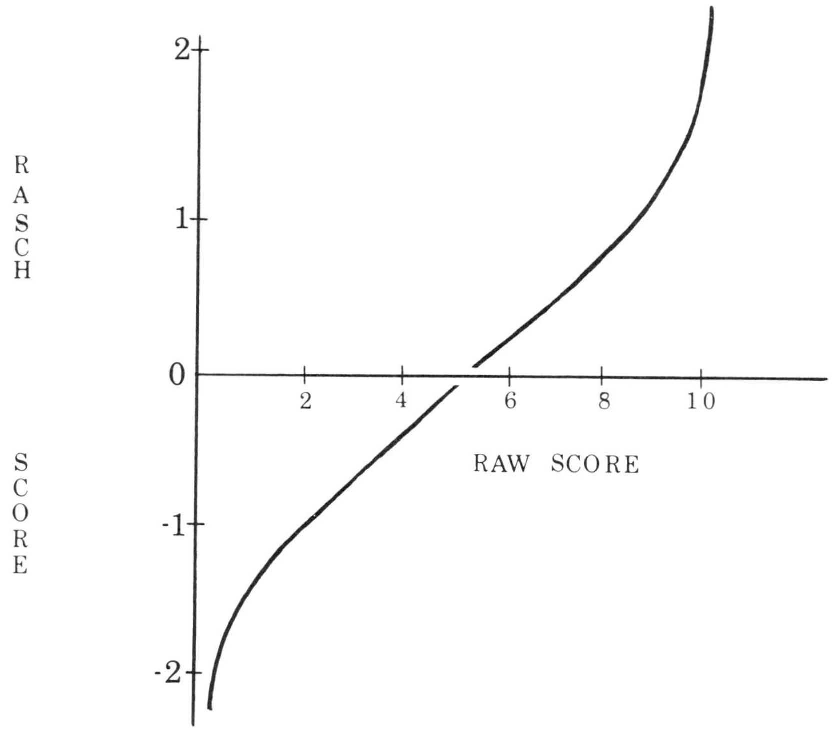

Source: Constructed by the author.

24

the scaled score is the sum of the dichotomously coded (correct/incorrect) item responses (Nunnally 1967; Guilford 1954). Therefore, traditional reliability estimates such as Cronbach's alpha and the Kuder- Richardson formulas may not be applicable to Rasch tests.

The Hoyt index has been used to estimate the reliability of Rasch tests (Whitely and Dawis 1974; Bring 1972; Hambleton and Traub 1973). This coefficient is calculated using an item by subject analysis of the variance model (Hoyt 1941; Thorndike 1971; Stanley 1957b). The procedure used to calculate this coefficient is described in C. J. Hoyt (1941).

The procedure for selecting items for inclusion in a Rasch test has been described. Items are considered for inclusion if the fit mean squares are less than $F(N - 1, \infty)$ and the discrimination indices are within three standard errors of the discrimination index of unity. The problems concerning the assessment of the internal consistency reliability of Rasch tests using traditional techniques such as Cronbach's alpha and the Kuder-Richardson formulas also have been presented. The use of Hoyt's analysis of variance procedure has been advocated. The current state of the research concerning Rasch tests will be described in the next section.

CURRENT RESEARCH CONCERNING THE RASCH MODEL

The literature germane to the Rasch model can be partitioned into four areas: (1) the underlying theory (Anderson 1973; Kifer, Mattson, and Carlid 1975; Hambleton and Cook 1976; Wright and Douglas 1974; Wright and Panchapakesan 1969); (2) parameter estimation (Wright and Panchapakesan 1969; Wright and Mead 1975; Kifer, Mattson, and Carlid 1975; Anderson 1973); (3) procedures for constructing Rasch tests (Ingebo 1976; Arneklev, Gee, and Ingebo 1976; Kifer, Mattson, and Carlid 1975; Wright and Mead 1975); and (4) the invariance properties (Forster 1976; Forbes and Ingebo 1975; Anderson, Kearney, and Everett 1968; Willmott and Fowles 1974; Mead 1974; Whitely and Dawis 1974, 1976).

The work concerning the theory underlying the Rasch model and procedures for constructing Rasch tests have been outlined previously. The reader interested in a detailed account of the parameter estimation procedures is referred to more detailed treatises of that topic (Wright and Panchapakesan 1969; Wright and Mead 1975; Kifer, Mattson, and Carlid 1975; Anderson 1973).

Research reported to date has centered around two major properties: test score invariance and item difficulty invariance. The remaining two sections of this chapter will be devoted to a discussion of the research concerning these two properties.

Rasch Item Difficulty Invariance

The Rasch procedure assumes that both items and subjects occupy positions on the same latent trait dimension. The position of an item is defined as the item's difficulty within the context of the Rasch model. The item difficulty invariance means that the position of an item on the latent dimension is not a function of the sample of subjects used to obtain estimates of that position.

F. Forster (1976) has attempted to determine the minimum sized calibration sample necessary to obtain stable item difficulty estimates. The data for his study were obtained from a sample of 1,478 fourth-grade and 1,808 eighth-grade students. These students had taken part in the Portland testing program in fourth-grade mathematics and eighth-grade reading. Forty samples of students were selected. Five samples each of 50, 100, 200, and 300 subjects were randomly selected from each of the fourth- and eighth-grade populations. Rasch item difficulty estimates were calculated using each of the 20 samples within each grade and the total populations for each grade as calibration groups.

Forster used the Pearsonian product moment correlation coefficient as the stability criterion. The product moment coefficient was calculated between calibration groups across items (the item was the unit of analysis). He reports correlations of item difficulty estimates between samples ranging from a low of .9471 to a high of .9910. The average correlation was .9797. The largest fluctuations in item difficulty estimates were with calibration samples of between 50 and 100 subjects in size. His results indicate that sample sizes of 150 to 200 subjects are required to obtain stable item difficulty estimates.

Forbes and Ingebo (1975) have reported the results of a study of the Rasch item difficulty invariance property. They were attempting to test directly the invariance property. Unlike Forster, they were not concerned with minimum sample size. Forbes and Ingebo used seventh-grade arithmetic item data. The items were prescreened using traditional difficulty and discrimination criteria. The items that satisfied the traditional criteria were calibrated using the Rasch procedure using each of 12 different groups of subjects. They report rank difference correlations of 1.0 between the Rasch item difficulty estimates obtained for the same set of items from each of the 12 groups.

J. Anderson, G. E. Kearney, and A. V. Everett (1968) report that they obtained high Pearson correlations between the Rasch item difficulty estimates obtained for prescreened items and using two groups of subjects. The subjects were divided into a high and a low group on the basis of the total test score. Item difficulty estimates for each item were obtained for each of the samples.

A. S. Willmott and D. E. Fowles (1974) also investigated the item difficulty invariance property. They used traditionally screened physics, mathematics, geography, and English test items. Two groups of subjects (a high and a low group) were selected on the basis of the total test score. They report bivariate plots of Rasch item difficulties for the same sets of items using each of the two groups as calibration samples. Although the plots reported by Willmott and Fowles seem to describe a linear trend, no correlation indices were reported. Data sufficient for the calculation of the correlation between item difficulties for one test (English) were reported. The correlation between item difficulties obtained from the high and low groups for the English test items selected by the Rasch procedure, as reported by Hashway (1977), was .9727. The slope of the regression of high-group item difficulties on low-group difficulties was 1.026 (Hashway 1977). The theoretical value of the regression parameter is 1.0. (The use of the regression procedure in this context will be discussed later.)

Although the correlation of .9727 and the bivariate graphs reported by Willmott and Fowles are impressive, the observed item difficulties for each group and item were not reported. Therefore, it is difficult to make any definitive statements concerning item difficulty invariance.

The empirical research reported above has concerned the item difficulty invariance property of the Rash model. These attempts to study empirically the item difficulty invariance property can be criticized on at least two points. First, some of these studies present as evidence nothing more than bivariate plots (Willmott and Fowles 1974). Without some type of test statistic, one cannot ascertain whether or not the differences observed between item difficulty estimates are significant or merely due to chance. The inspection of a bivariate plot is not sufficient to test the item difficulty invariance property. Second, the correlation coefficient is not the appropriate statistic.

Some researchers have reported Pearsonian correlations between item difficulty estimates (Anderson, Kearney, and Everett 1968; Forster 1976). Others have reported rank difference correlations between item difficulty estimates (Forbes and Ingebo 1975). The major statistical difference between these two correlational indices is that the Pearsonian assumes that the variables being correlated are sampled from a universe population that is normally distributed (the Pearsonian) where the rank difference correlation makes no distributional assumptions. The reader interested in these differences between the two types of correlation coefficients is referred to the nonparametric statistics literature (Hollander and Wolfe 1973;

Kendall 1970; Conover 1971). The major issue is not with the type of coefficient calculated, however; rather it is that the correlation coefficient is not the appropriate statistic (Hashway 1977).

The correlation coefficient is a measure of rank order invariance. If a group of items maintains the same relative rank order based on difficulty estimates across calibration groups, the correlation coefficients (both Pearsonian and rank order) will be high. If items do not maintain the same or similar relative rank orders, both types of correlation coefficients will be low. The item difficulty invariance property requires that the item difficulty estimates be numerically the same for the same item across calibration samples. The existence of a high correlation, or similar rank orders of items across calibration samples, is a necessary but not sufficient test of the invariance property. If item difficulty estimates are similar across samples, the rank order of items based on the estimates will be similar (that is, high correlations). The existence of similar rank orders, however, does not imply equivalence of raw scores (McNemar 1962; Ferguson 1971).

Given this level of specificity, the question now becomes, What is (are) a sufficient statistic(s) for the test of the item difficulty invariance property? Fortunately, this question is easily answered. Consider the same set of items calibrated using two different groups of subjects. The difficulty estimate obtained for item i using groups j and k will be symbolized by d_{ij} and d_{ik}, respectively. If the item difficulty invariance property is operative in the data, the two difficulty estimates should be equivalent. Consider the regression equation between the item difficulty estimates, written as follows:

$$d_{ik} = b_1 d_{ij} + b_2 \qquad (2.3)$$

The parameters b_1 and b_2 are called the slope and intercept parameters, respectively. These parameters are estimated using least squares procedures (McNemar 1962) for more than one Rasch item and two calibration samples. If the item difficulty estimates are equivalent across calibration samples, the regression equation obtained from the item difficulties should not be different from the equation $d_{ik} = (1.0) d_{ij} + 0.0$. The sufficient condition required to conclude that the item invariance property is operant is that b_1 is not significantly different from 1.0 and that b_2 is not significantly different from 0.0.

The sufficient statistic for testing the hypothesis that $b_1 = 1$ and $b_2 = 0$ is the t-statistic. The t-statistic used is the quotient of the difference between the hypothesized and observed regression coefficients divided by the standard error of the regression coefficient (Heald 1969; McNemar 1972; Winter 1971; Worthing and Giffner 1943).

The regression procedure tests the property that item difficulty should be invariant across calibration samples.

S. E. Whitely and R. V. Dawis (1976) report an alternative approach to testing the item difficulty invariance property. They used a sample of 1,568 students enrolled in two Minneapolis suburban high school systems. A 60-item verbal analogy test was utilized. The 60 items had been traditionally prescreened using a sample of high school and college students (Tinsley 1971). Using the prescreen item pool, they found 15 items that satisfied the Rasch model assumptions. Seven alternative forms were constructed, each of which consisted of the 15 Rasch items and 45 items of similar substantive content. Each of the seven forms was administered to high school students. The number of students that were administered each form ranged from 210 to 241. Item difficulty estimates for each of the original 15 items were obtained using the data for each form. Because there were seven forms, seven item difficulty estimates, one using each form, were obtained for each item. Whitely and Dawis concluded that item difficulty invariance was a function of the environment of the other items with which the 15 Rasch items were combined.

To examine their data, Whitely and Dawis used a particular type of one-way analysis of variance procedure. The unit of analysis was the item, the dependent variable was the item difficulty estimate obtained using each of the seven test forms, and the independent variable was the particular form used to determine the item difficulty estimate (one factor with seven levels). The within-cell variance was estimated by "the squared standard errors weighted by N" (Whitely and Dawis 1976, p. 334). The validity of the procedure rests on the assumption that they are correct in their choice of procedure for the calculation of the within-cell variance. No rationale or reference relative to their choice of the within-cell error term was cited by Whitely and Dawis. Thus, their procedure is at best questionable at this point.

The Whitely and Dawis data were reanalyzed by this author (Hashway 1977). The average rank difference correlation across forms of item difficulty was .99. The Whitely-Dawis data, when analyzed in this fashion, seem to negate the conclusions arrived at by the original investigators and to agree with the results reported by Forbes and Ingebo (1975), who report rank difference correlations of 1.00. It seems that Rasch item difficulty estimates obtained from either different samples or different forms tend to rank order items in the same way.

It was argued previously that the preservation of rank order is a necessary but not sufficient condition for item difficulty invariance. Therefore, the next step was to calculate the slopes of the Rasch item difficulty regression lines. Using the Whitely-Dawis data, the slopes were calculated by Hashway (1977). The averages of the slopes (b_1) and intercepts (b_2) of the regression lines were 1.02 and .03, respectively. Each of the slopes and intercepts was tested for significant departure from unity or zero, respectively, using a t-statistic (Heald 1969; Winer 1971; Worthing and Giffner 1943; McNemar 1962). None of the slopes was found to be significantly different from 1.0 (p less than .01) and none of the intercepts was found to be significantly different from 0 (p less than .01).

Therefore, the Whitely-Dawis data can be seen as confirming the invariance of Rasch item difficulty estimates and that invariance is not a function of the items that may be combined with the Rasch items as the original investigators had concluded. Hashway's reanalysis tends to indicate that there may be a serious problem with the Whitely-Dawis procedure. Perhaps the problem may lie in the selection of the procedure for the calculation of the within-cell variance.

Rasch Score Invariance

In addition to the invariance of item difficulty over calibration populations, the Rasch model purports to possess another interesting property: the invariance of score estimates. The score associated with particular people should be invariant with respect to variations of the items constituting the test upon which that score was based. Specifically, given two tests where the items constituting each test were selected from the same set of Rasch-calibrated items, the scores obtained by the same individual from both tests should not differ by any more than that which would be expected from random error alone.

Some authors have interpreted score invariance to mean that the same total score (number of items answered correctly) obtained from each of two Rasch tests should correspond to the same Rasch score (Doherty and Forster 1976; Wright and Douglas 1974; Wright 1967). This interpretation implies that subject A, who responds correctly to two items on Rasch test A, should be given the same Rasch score as subject B, who responded correctly to two items on Rasch test B. It has been found that the number of correct responses versus Rasch score formulas for two tests constructed from the same item pool correspond quite well (Doherty and Forster 1976; Wright and Douglas 1974; Wright 1967).

Wright (1967) administered the 48-item reading comprehension subtest of the Law School Admission Test to 976 beginning law students. Twenty-four of the easiest items were used to construct one test and the remaining 24 more difficult items constituted a second test. The average number of items answered correctly were 17.16 (standard deviation = 3.93) and 10.38 (standard deviation = 4.29) using the easy and hard tests, respectively. The mean Rasch test scores using the easy and hard tests were .464 (standard deviation = .997) and .403 (standard deviation = .868), respectively. In addition, Wright demonstrated that the same total score obtained using two different tests corresponded to virtually identical Rasch log ability estimates.

Score invariance is more general than described above. Another dimension of score invariance is that the Rasch scores associated with a particular person obtained from any two or more tests whose items were selected from a calibrated set of items will be statistically equivalent (Wright and Panchapakesan 1969; Whitely and Dawis 1974).

A major issue is what is a sufficient statistic for testing this more general score invariance property. B. E. A. Tinsley (1971), using classical statistics, concluded that the ability estimates obtained from Rasch tests were not invariant over item subsets. Whitely and Dawis (1974) point out that the classical statistical procedures tend to confound the precision of measurement with statistical equivalency. Tests of statistical equivalency (classical) are not designed to take into account known errors of measurement or limits to precision.

Whitely and Dawis go on to point out that a test of score equivalence must take into account the precision of the instrument used to make the measurements. Because tests consist of a finite number of items, the measurement made using a test contains a certain amount of imprecision. The estimate of this uncertainty or imprecision associated with Rasch tests is the standard error of the ability estimate.

The test statistic proposed by Wright (1967) accounts for the variations inherent in the instrument by means of the standard error of the ability estimate. This measure is called the standardized difference score (Whitely and Dawis 1974). Assume that the Rasch scores obtained by person p from tests 1 and 2 are x_{1p} and x_{2p}, respectively. The standard error of the ability estimates corresponding to the scores x_{1p} and x_{2p} will be symbolized by $SE(x_{1p})$ and $SE(x_{2p})$, respectively. The standardized difference score for person p, z_p, is defined in terms of Equation 2.4 (Whitely and Dawis 1974):

$$z_p = (x_{1p} - x_{2p})(SE(x_{2p})^2 + SE(x_{1p})^2)^{-\frac{1}{2}} \qquad (2.4)$$

The standardized difference score is interpreted as a z-score (Whitely and Dawis 1974). The distribution of the population from which z_p is sampled is assumed to be normally distributed with zero mean and unit variance. The standardized difference statistic is traceable to Wright (1967).

The present author (Hashway 1977) feels that Wright overlooked an important consideration. If the error is exactly what would be expected from random error alone, z_p can be considered to be sampled from $N(0,1)$. However, if the observed score differences are <u>less</u> than what would be considered to be attributable to random error alone, the standardized difference score would be sampled from a normally distributed population, $N(0, s^2)$, where $s < 1$. If the observed score differences are <u>greater</u> than what would be considered to arise from random error alone, the population distribution of z_p would be $N(\bar{Z}, s^2)$ where $\bar{Z} \neq 0$ <u>or</u> $s > 1$. Therefore, although the results reported by Whitely and Dawis tend to agree with their assertion that z_p is sampled from $N(0,1)$ that assertion is generally false.

The Wright procedure (1967) is to sum the standardized difference scores over the population and test this sum for significant departure from zero. The traditional test is the t-test (Winer 1971). The sum of a finite number, N, of unit normal deviates follows a t-distribution with $N - 1$ degrees of freedom (Harris 1966). However, if the sample distribution is anything other than unit normal, the test assumptions are not satisfied.

Hashway (1977) reports the results of a study of the Rasch item-free property. He used a sample of about 2,000 students from the Republic of Ireland and two tests constructed from a criterion-referenced mathematics test that had not been previously psychometrically prescreened. It was found that the distribution of the standardized difference statistic was not normally distributed, and the variance of the distribution was much less than one. Hashway's results indicate that Rasch tests constructed from nontraditionally prescreened item pools are more error-free and correspond more closely to the properties of the Rasch model than tests constructed from traditionally prescreened item pools.

There is another critical problem with the Wright procedure. It is possible for the procedure to indicate that two tests are equivalent when in fact the score for the same person on one test is the algebraic opposite of the person's score on another test. Consider the set of scores in Table 2.1. The mean and variance of the standardized difference scores are 0 and 1, respectively. Therefore, using the Wright procedure, the conclusion is that these tests are equivalent. The distribution of scores in Table 2.1 clearly indicates that the two tests are definitely not equivalent. Although the example cited contained only two cases, all that is necessary to show that a procedure is erroneous is one counterexample. The scores for two tests resulting in quite opposite results but that satisfy the Wright equivalence criterion can be easily generated for any number of cases.

Although there are problems with the current significance tests surrounding the standardized difference score, a method of testing

TABLE 2.1

A Hypothetical Distribution of Rasch Test Scores
for Two Individuals and Two Tests

Subject	Test Score		Standardized Difference Statistic, t_i
	Test 1	Test 2	
1	-.3536	.3536	.7072
2	.3536	-.3536	-.7072
Mean	.0000	.0000	.0000
Variance (unbiased)	.5000	.5000	1.0000

Source: Compiled by the author.

the score invariance property of the Rasch model using these scores
can be developed. As stated previously, the major issue concerning
the testing of any hypothesis is, What is the sufficient statistic? In
the course of this research a procedure for testing the score invariance property using the distribution of Wright's (1967) standardized
difference scores was developed (Hashway 1977). The procedure
resulted in a set of sufficient statistics for testing the score invariance property. That procedure and the sufficient statistics will now
be described.

The definition of score invariance can be restated in terms of
the standardized difference score. The standardized difference score
and the procedure used for its calculation have been described previously (see Equation 2.4). Two tests are said to be score invariant if
the observed distribution of standardized difference scores can be
explained by at most random error. This definition renders a solution
to the problem of the choice of a sufficient statistic.

The procedure proposed for testing the score invariance property
involves observing the distribution of standardized difference scores.
This is essentially a two-step process. The first step is to compare
the observed distribution with the normal distribution function. The
second step is to determine the nature of the departure from normal-
ity. If it is found that the standardized difference score is due to
random error, the score invariance property is operant and the
second step can be omitted.

The comparison between the observed distribution of standardized difference scores and the expected normal distribution function
can be performed using either the chi-square or Komolgorov-Smirnov

FIGURE 2.4   Hypothesized Frequency Polygons of the Standardized Difference Score

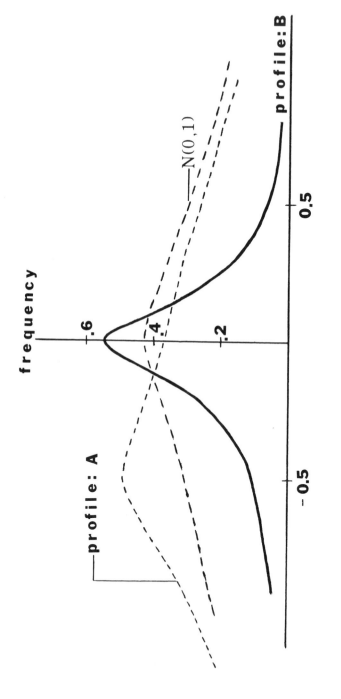

Source: Constructed by the author.

statistics (Conover 1971; Hollander and Wolfe 1973). F. J. Massey (1951) reports some indication that the Komolgorov-Smirnov test is more sensitive to departures from the expected distribution than the chi-square test. However, Massey's simulation was performed with large samples of subjects but a small population of samples (46). Therefore, the existing evidence in favor of the Komolgorov-Smirnov test over chi-square is not impressive. It is suggested that both tests be used. If the Komolgorov-Smirnov or chi-square test achieves significance, the hypothesis that the standardized difference scores are distributed as the unit normal should be rejected. If the hypothesis that the observed distribution is similar to the unit normal distribution is rejected, the second step in the procedure should be performed.

There are two reasons why the observed distribution would be non-normal: First, the observed variation may be greater than expected assuming a normal distribution of error. This situation will result in a probability distribution profile similar to curve A in Figure 2.4. The number of concordant test scores will be fewer and the number of discordant test scores will be greater than expected from the error function. Second, the observed variation may be in greater concordance with the Rasch score invariance property than would be expected from normal error functions. This situation will result in a profile similar to curve B in Figure 2.4. The number of concordant scores would be greater and the number of discordant test scores would be fewer than expected from the error function.

If it is assumed that two tests result in Rasch scores that are in greater concordance than expected from random error when three properties are present: the frequency of standardized difference scores centered about zero must be greater than expected from random error alone, thereby indicating a larger than expected frequency of concordant test scores, the frequency of standardized difference scores at the extreme ends of the distribution must be less than expected from the error function and these frequencies should approach $N(0, 1)$ asymptotically as the value of the observed difference score increases (the second property indicates that the number of discordant scores is less than expected from the error function); and the variance of the standardized difference score should be significantly less than 1.0 (the third property ensures that the dispersion of difference scores is less than expected from random error alone).

The first two properties can be determined by examining the observed and expected frequency distributions. The third property can be verified with an F_{max}-test (Winer 1971). If any of the three properties are found not to be operative, the score invariance property of the Rasch model can be said not to be verified. Otherwise, the score invariance property of the Rasch model can be said to be operant and the observed score differences, at most, are due to random error.

The empirical research performed to date and concerning the properties of the Rasch model have been discussed. The results seem on the surface to verify the existence of the Rasch invariance properties. However, as it has been pointed out, certain problems exist concerning the statistics used in these studies. New statistical procedures have been presented, which, perhaps more directly, test the properties of the Rasch model.

3

INFERENCES AND COMPARISONS
AT THE INDIVIDUAL LEVEL

The material presented in this chapter concerns inferences and comparisons that can be made between individuals and relative to a particular individual tested using two tests or the same test on two occasions. The mathematical details as well as examples of the application of each procedure are presented. This chapter contains four major sections. The first section presents a model of Rasch test scores in terms of true scores and measurement error. The second section describes transformations that can be performed on Rasch test scores while retaining the interval scale structure of Rasch scales. The next section describes a model for testing the significance of change for a particular individual over time or between equivalent tests. The final section describes procedures for making inferences and ratio-level comparisons between individuals and two or more test scores obtained for the same individual.

A MODEL OF RASCH TEST SCORES
AS TRUE SCORE ESTIMATES

Rasch test scores have been referred to as tau, or true score, equivalent scores (Whitely and Dawis 1974; Wright 1967). This means that an equation can be written between observed Rasch test scores and true scores. (Reference to this conceptualization of Rasch test scores has been made in the previous chapter.) This section is an elaboration and specification of the theory originally presented by Whitely and Dawis and Wright.

What Are True Scores?

It was pointed out in the previous chapter that an index called the standard error of the estimate is associated with each Rasch test score. The standard error associated with a particular measurement is a measure of the error inherent in that measurement. For the purposes here, a true score is a measurement with a standard error numerically equal to zero. True scores are conceptualized as Rasch measurements, or equivalently, positions on the same dimension as the observed Rasch measurement, which are determined without error. Because such an error-free measurement exists in theory alone, it is necessary to associate the observed Rasch measurement with a corresponding true score and error term. The association is the purpose of the fundamental measurement model.

The Fundamental Measurement Model

There are three components or sources of variation associated with a particular Rasch test score. One component is the observed test score. For the purposes of notational continuity, the Rasch test score will be symbolized by the letter z. A second component of a Rasch test score is the true score for which the observed test score is an estimate. True scores will be symbolized by the Greek letter μ. The third component is the error of measurement, e. The error of measurement is a measure of the departure of the observed test score, z, from the true score, μ. The error component, e, is assumed to be normally distributed with a mean of zero and a standard deviation equal to the standard error of measurement. The standard error of measurement associated with a particular Rasch test score, z, will be symbolized by s(z).

The Rasch measurement model is a summative model of true scores and errors of measurements. An observed score, z, is conceptualized as being the sum of the true score, μ, and an error score, e. Again, the error of measurement, e, is assumed to be normally distributed with a mean of zero and a standard deviation equal to the standard error of measurement, s(z). Symbolically, the summative relation between a particular Rasch test score, z, the associated true score, μ, and an error term, e, can be written in terms of an elementary equation:

$$z = \mu + e \qquad\qquad (3.1)$$

where

$$e \sim \mathcal{N}(0, s^2(z))$$

The equation above will be called the fundamental measurement model. The fundamental measurement model explicitly states that an observed score is composed of two components: true score and error. It also specifies the distributional character of the error term: normal with a mean of zero and a standard deviation equal to the standard error of measurement.

Useful Properties of the Fundamental Measurement Model

The fundamental measurement model has certain properties and implications that are useful for making inferences about Rasch test scores. These properties and implications evolve from the specification of the distribution of the error term. The fundamental measurement model results in procedures by which inferences can be made concerning the difference between any two Rasch scores as well as the difference between any two groups of Rasch observed test scores. The mathematical details concerning inferences relative to two scores obtained for an individual or two different individuals will be presented in this section. Mathematical details concerning inferences relative to groups of individuals is somewhat more complex and will be discussed in Chapter 4. Examples of the application of the model will be made in subsequent sections of this chapter and in the following chapters.

Inferences Concerning Two Rasch Measurements

Consider two Rasch measurements z_1 and z_2 with the associated standard errors of s_1 and s_2, respectively. These measurements may arise from a number of possible situations. One situation may be that a particular student was administered two equivalent tests at the same testing. A second situation may arise from the administration of a particular test or two equivalent tests at two different times to the same student. In addition, a third situation is the administration of a particular test to two students at the same time. Assume that the two observed scores z_1 and z_2 are not equal $(z_2 - z_1 \neq 0)$. The inferential question is whether or not the observed score difference is sufficiently large to imply that a nonzero true score difference $(\mu_2 - \mu_1 \neq 0)$ exists. A procedure for addressing this inferential problem will be presented in this section.

If z_1 and z_2 are observed Rasch scores with the associated standard errors of s_1 and s_2, then the fundamental measurement model implies that there exists true scores μ_1 and μ_2 as well as error scores e_1 and e_2 such that each observed score is equal to the sum of the respective error and true scores. The relations between observed true and error scores can be written in terms of the following equations:

$$z_1 = \mu_1 + e_1 \tag{3.2}$$

$$z_2 = \mu_2 + e_2 \tag{3.3}$$

where

$$e_1 \sim \mathcal{N}(0, s_1^2) \quad \text{and} \quad e_2 \sim \mathcal{N}(0, s_2^2)$$

Consider the difference between the two observed scores $(z_2 - z_1)$. That difference can be expressed in terms of a true score difference $(\mu_1 - \mu_2)$ and a difference in error terms $(e_2 - e_1)$ by subtracting Equation 3.2 from 3.3:

$$z_2 - z_1 = (\mu_2 - \mu_1) + (e_2 - e_1) \tag{3.4}$$

where

$$(e_2 - e_1) \sim \mathcal{N}(0, s^2) \quad \text{and} \quad s^2 = s_1^2 + s_2^2$$

If the difference between observed scores is zero $(z_2 - z_1 = 0)$, then any true score difference is due to random error (the null hypothesis). Consequently, numerically equivalent observed scores imply equivalent true scores.

Consider the case where the observed scores are not equal $(z_1 - z_2 \neq 0)$. This is by far the more interesting case. Again, the issue is whether or not the observed score difference $(z_2 - z_1 \neq 0)$ is sufficient to infer that a nonzero true score difference $(\mu_2 - \mu_1 \neq 0)$ exists. The null hypothesis is that the true scores are not different. The statement that the difference between true scores is zero $(\mu_2 - \mu_1 = 0)$ is equivalent to the null hypothesis. Making the substitution $\mu_2 - \mu_1 = 0$ into Equation 3.4 yields the following result:

$$z_2 - z_1 = e_2 - e_1 \tag{3.5}$$

where

$$(e_2 - e_1) \sim \mathcal{N}(0, s^2) \quad \text{and} \quad s^2 = s_1^2 + s_2^2$$

Therefore, if the null hypothesis is to be accepted, the difference between observed scores must be no greater than what would be expected from a random variable which is sampled from a normally distributed population with a mean of zero and a variance of $s_1^2 + s_2^2$.

If both sides of Equation 3.5 are divided by $(s_1^2 + s_2^2)^{\frac{1}{2}}$, the following result is obtained.

$$\xi = \frac{z_2 - z_1}{s} = \frac{e_2 - e_1}{s} \sim \mathcal{N}(0,1) \tag{3.6}$$

where

$$s^2 = s_1^2 + s_2^2$$

The quantity ξ, defined by Equation 3.6, corresponds to the Whitely and Dawis (1974) standardized difference statistic. For inferential purposes, the ξ index will be called the test statistic.

If the null hypothesis is accepted, the test statistic, ξ, is normally distributed with a mean of zero and unit variance. Therefore, if ξ is no greater than expected from a unit normal random variable, the null hypothesis is accepted. The expected value of ξ and the associated confidence bands are 1.96 (p = .95), 3.29 (p = .99), and 3.89 (p = .999). If ξ is greater (less) than 1.96, the null hypothesis is rejected (accepted) with 95 percent confidence. If ξ is greater (less) than 3.29, the null hypothesis is rejected (accepted) with a confidence limit of 99 percent. If the value of ξ is greater (less) than 3.89, the null hypothesis is rejected (accepted) with a confidence limit of one part in a thousand. If the null hypothesis is accepted, the substantive inference is that the observed score difference is due to measurement error and is not sufficiently large to imply the existence of a true score difference. If the null hypothesis is rejected, the substantive inference is that the observed score difference is greater than expected from random error and is sufficiently large to imply the existence of a significant true score difference (nonzero).

The mathematical details of the fundamental measurement model have been presented in this section. The model has been extended to inferences between two individual level measurements. Further extensions of the basic model to experimental designs will be presented in Chapter 4. The remainder of this chapter will be devoted to discussions of the interpretation of individual level test results and applications of the inferential procedures discussed. One section is devoted to a discussion of the interpretation of the scores of a particular individual from two equivalent tests, or the same test at two different points in time. The next section concerns inferences that can be made on the basis of individual scores. The final section of this chapter deals with inferences that can be made relative to test scores obtained by two individuals.

THE TRANSFORMATION OF INDIVIDUAL
RASCH TEST SCORES

The range of Rasch test scores is, in theory, unlimited. Any number between negative infinity and positive infinity can be valid logarithmic Rasch scores. This point was discussed in Chapter 2. Rasch test scores (logarithmic) may take integer values (positive or negative), such as +3, -4, +200, -40, and so on, or rational values, such as -3.62, 4.17, -27.643, 78.964, and so forth. The range of possible values a traditional test score can assume is in one-to-one correspondence with the set of positive integers starting with zero and increasing to a maximum equal to the number of items composing the test. Scores obtained from a traditional test containing 10 items are equivalent or identical to the 11 whole numbers: 0, 1, 2, 3, ... 8, 9, 10. The Rasch model results in test scores that are quite different from well-known traditional test scores. Because Rasch test scores are interval scale measurements, various transformations can be performed on the test scores. These transformations map Rasch scores onto scales currently used for reporting traditional test scores and are more well known than the original (untransformed) Rasch scores. These transformations do not change the interval character of the Rasch scale.

Four types of transformed scores will be discussed in this section: standardized scores, T-scores, SAT-scores, and W-score. Standardized scores are test scores that are distributed with a mean of zero and unit variance. The T-score is distributed with a mean of 50 and a standard deviation of 10. The SAT-score is distributed with a mean of 500 and a standard deviation of 100. The W-scale score

TABLE 3.1

The Mean and Standard Deviations of Each of Four Transformed Distributions

	Logarithmic Untransformed	Standardized	T-Scores	SAT	W-Scale*
Mean	$\bar{Z}$	0	50	500	$a_W \bar{Z} + b_W$
Standard deviation	S	1	10	100	$a_W S$

*$a_W = 9.1024$ and $b_W = 100$.

Source: Compiled by the author.

TABLE 3.2

Transformation Constants

Constant	Type of Transformation			
	Standardized	T–Score	SAT–Score	W–Scale Score
a	$1/S$	$10/S$	$100/S$	9.1024
b	$-\bar{Z}/S$	$50 - (10\,\bar{Z}/S)$	$500 - (100\,\bar{Z}/S)$	100.0000

Source: Compiled by the author.

was developed by R. W. Woodcock and M. N. Dahl (1976) in collaboration with Benjamin Wright of the University of Chicago. If the mean and standard deviation of the original untransformed Rasch scores are $\bar{Z}$ and S, respectively, the W–scores are distributed with a mean of $0.1024\,\bar{Z} + 100$ and a standard deviation of 9.1024 S. The mean and standard deviation of each of the transformed distributions are shown in Table 3.1.

The transformation of a particular Rasch score to any of the four scales defined above is accomplished by means of what is called a linear affine transformation mathematically. If F(z) is the transformed score corresponding to the untransformed score z, and $\bar{Z}$ and S are the mean and standard deviation, respectively, of the untransformed Rasch scores, the relation between F(z) and z is defined by the following equation:

$$F(z) = az + b \qquad (3.7)$$

The values of a and b are constant for a particular transformation and a particular set of untransformed Rasch test results. The values of the constants a and b for each transformation are shown in Table 3.2.

The standard error, $SE_F(z)$, of the transformed score, F(z), is not equat to the standard error, s(z), of the untransformed Rasch score, z. The following equation describes the relationship between the standard errors of transformed and untransformed standard errors:

$$SE_F(z) = a\,s(z) \qquad (3.8)$$

TABLE 3.3

An Exemplary Distribution of Rasch Test Scores

Rasch Test Score (Logarithmic)	Standard Error
-4.99	3.33
-1.65	1.11
- .72	.88
.00	.83
.71	.88
1.66	1.11
4.99	3.33
Mean Rasch test score	.8073
Standard deviation	2.1537

Source: Compiled by the author.

The remainder of this section will present examples of these transformations, with a particular set of Rasch test scores used for each example. This data set corresponds to a particular six-item Rasch test. The Rasch scores and associated standard errors are shown in Table 3.3.

Transformation to Standard Scores

Rasch test scores can be transformed to what have been known as standardized scores. These standardized scores are distributed with a mean or average of zero and a standard deviation of 1.0. Equation 3.7 can be used to accomplish this transformation. The values of the constants a and b can be determined by using the formulas in the first column of Table 3.2. Because the constant a is defined by the equation $a = 1.0/S$, and the standard deviation of the Rasch test scores shown in Table 3.3 is 2.1537, the value of the constant is $a = 1.0/2.1537$, or 0.4643. Because the formula for the constant b is $b = -\bar{Z}/S$, and the mean ($\bar{Z}$) and standard deviation (S) of the Rasch test scores shown in Table 3.3 are .8073 and 2.1537, respectively, the value of the constant b is $-(.8073/2.1537)$, or $-.3748$. Once the values of the transformation constants have been determined, these values may be substituted directly into Equation 3.7 to obtain the desired transformation equation. For this particular example, the transformation equation is given by Equation 3.9:

$$F(z) = 0.4643\,z - .3748 \tag{3.9}$$

Equation 3.8 can be used to define the relation between the standard errors of the transformed (SE_F) and untransformed (s) Rasch test scores. The equation that describes the relation between the standard errors for this particular example is

$$SE_F(z) = 0.4643\,s(z) \tag{3.10}$$

Consider the Rasch test score of -.72 with a standard error of .88 (see Table 3.4). The transformed Rasch score can be found by using Equation 3.9:

$$F(-.72) = (0.4643) \cdot (-.72)) - .3748 = -.7091 \tag{3.11}$$

The standard error of the transformed Rasch score can be found by using Equation 3.10.

$$SE_F(-.72) = (0.4643) \cdot (0.88) = 0.4086 \tag{3.12}$$

The standardized transformations of each of the Rasch scores described by Table 3.3 are shown in Table 3.4.

Transformation to T-Scores

Rasch test results can be transformed to T-scores. T-scores are distributed with a mean of 50 and a standard deviation of 10.0. Equation 3.7 is used to transform the Rasch test scores. The values of the parameters a and b can be found by using the formulas shown in Table 3.2. The value of the first parameter, a, is 10/S, or 10.0/2.1537, or 4.6432. The value of the second parameter, b, is $50 - (10\bar{Z}/S) = 50 - (10(.8073)/2.1537) = 50 - 3.7484 = 46.2516$. Therefore, the equations transforming Rasch test scores and their associated standard errors to T-scores and T-standard errors can be found by substituting the values of parameters a and b, whose values were determined from the sample data, into Equations 3.7 and 3.8, respectively. The results of the substitutions are

$$F(z) = 4.6432\,Z + 46.2516 \tag{3.13}$$

$$SE_F(z) = 4.6432\,s(z) \tag{3.14}$$

TABLE 3.4

An Example of the Transformation of Rasch Test Results to Standardized Test Scores

| Untransformed | | Type of Test Score | Transformed | |
Observed Score	Standard Error	Standard Score	Transformed	Standard Error
Z	s(Z)	$.4643\,Z - .7348 = F(z)$		$.4643\,s(z) = SE_F(z)$
-4.99	3.33	$.4643(-4.99) - .7348 = -3.05$		$.4643(3.33) = 1.55$
-1.65	1.11	$.4643(-1.65) - .7348 = -1.50$		$.4643(1.11) = .52$
- .72	.88	$.4643(- .72) - .7348 = -1.07$		$.4643(.88) = .41$
.00	.83	$.4643(.00) - .7348 = - .73$		$.4643(.83) = .39$
.71	.88	$.4643(.71) - .7348 = - .41$		$.4643(.88) = .41$
1.66	1.11	$.4643(1.66) - .7348 = .04$		$.4643(1.11) = .52$
4.99	3.33	$.4643(4.99) - .7348 = 1.58$		$.4643(3.33) = 1.55$

Source: Compiled by the author.

46

Consider the untransformed Rasch test score of 1.66 with the associated standard error of 1.11 as shown in Table 3.3. Using Equation 3.13, the value of the T-score corresponding to that Rasch score is 4.6432(1.66) + 46.2516, or 53.9593. Using Equation 3.14, the standard error associated with a T-score of 53.9593 is 4.6432(1.11), or 5.1540. The T-scores and standard errors corresponding to the untransformed Rasch scores described in Table 3.3 are shown in Table 3.5.

Transformation to SAT-Scores

In addition to T-scores and standardized scores, Rasch measurements can also be transformed to SAT-scores. These transformed scores are distributed with a mean of 500 and a standard deviation of 100. As with the previous transformations, Equation 3.7 can be used to generate the transformation equation and the formulas for determining the required parameters (a and b) can be found by using Table 3.2. For the example shown in Table 3.3, the parameter a is equal to 100/2.1537, or 46.432. Parameter b is equal to 500 − (100(.8073/2.1537), or 462.516. The equations relating the SAT-transformed measurements and standard errors to the untransformed measurements and standard errors are found by substituting the values of the parameters a and b, found above, into Equations 3.7 and 3.8. The equations required to transform the data in Table 3.3 to SAT-scores are

$$F(z) = 46.432\,z + 462.516 \tag{3.15}$$

$$SE_F(z) = 46.432\,s(z) \tag{3.16}$$

The values of the transformed scores and standard errors corresponding to the data in Table 3.3 are shown in Table 3.5.

Transformations to the W-Scale

Woodcock and Dahl (1976) describe a particular transformation of Rasch test scores and their associated standard errors in terms of the following equations (transcribed into the current notation for convenience):

$$F(z) = 9.1024\,z + 100 \tag{3.17}$$

$$SE_F(z) = 9.1024\,s(z) \tag{3.18}$$

TABLE 3.5

Examples of Rasch Measurements After Transformation

| Untransformed | Standard Scores | Type of Transformation | | |
		T-Scores	SAT-Scores	W-Scale
-4.99(3.33)	-3.05(1.55)	23.08(15.46)	231 (155)	54.6(30.3)
-1.65(1.11)	-1.50(.52)	38.59(5.15)	386 (52)	84.9(10.1)
- .72(.88)	-1.07(.41)	42.91(4.09)	429 (41)	93.4(8.0)
.00(.83)	- .74(.39)	46.25(3.85)	463 (39)	100.0(7.6)
.71(.88)	- .41(.41)	49.55(4.09)	495 (41)	106.5(8.0)
1.66(1.11)	.04(.52)	53.96(5.15)	540 (51)	115.1(10.1)
4.99(3.33)	1.58(1.55)	69.42(15.46)	694 (155)	145.4(30.3)

Note: Standard errors are enclosed in parentheses.
Source: Compiled by the author.

Consider an untransformed Rasch score of -1.65 with an associated standard error of 1.11. The corresponding W-scale score is 9.1024(-1.65) + 100 = -15.0190 + 100, or 84.981. The standard error corresponding to a W-scale score of 84.981 (or, equivalently, an untransformed score of -1.65) is 9.1024(1.11), or 10.1037. The exemplary Rasch measurements and standard errors shown in Table 3.3 have been transformed to W-scale equivalents and these equivalents are shown in Table 3.5.

It has been pointed out that Rasch measurements may be transformed using an affine transformation without loss of the interval scaling property of the untransformed scale. Four types of transformed scales have been described: standardized, T-score, SAT-score, and W-scale. Procedures and formulas for transforming logarithmic Rasch scores and standard errors to particular measurement scales have also been presented. The remainder of this chapter will discuss the use of Rasch scores for making inferences with respect to particular individuals. It should be noted that if a transformed Rasch score and the associated transformed standard errors are used, the inferences obtained using the theory developed in the first section of this chapter or the procedures developed and discussed in the remainder of this chapter will be no different than if the untransformed Rasch measurement was used. The use of transformations is for the ease of human interpretability, and the inferential mathematics is not dependent upon the particular transformation (affine) selected. This last property is due to the fact that Rasch logarithmic measurements are made upon interval scales and that the interval scaling property of measurement scales is invariant under linear affine transformations. The transformations discussed in this section are all classifiable as linear affine transformations.

TESTING THE SIGNIFICANCE OF CHANGE SCORES

If a particular individual is administered a test on two distinct occasions and the scores assigned by these tests to that individual are not identical, two questions arise: (1) Is the difference in observed scores indicative of a difference in true scores? (2) Are the observed score differences due to measurement error? The purpose of this section is to present a procedure for testing the significance of observed differences in Rasch test scores obtained by the same individual from two or more tests. This section is organized in terms of three parts. The first part describes the mathematical model for assessing the significance of change scores. The second part presents examples of assessments of the significance of increases in test scores. The third part presents examples of the assessment of the significance of decreases in Rasch test scores.

The Mathematical Model of Individual Change

Let z_1 represent the Rasch test score for a particular individual at one point in time and s_1 correspond to the standard error associated with that Rasch score. Let z_2 represent the Rasch measurement for the same individual at a different point in time and s_2 correspond to the associated standard error. Let μ_1 and μ_2 represent the true scores corresponding to the Rasch observed measurements of z_1 and z_2, respectively. The fundamental measurement model can be applied to the data to obtain equations relating the observed and true scores as well as the error components, e_1 and e_2.

$$\left.\begin{array}{l} z_1 = \mu_1 + e_1 \\ \\ z_2 = \mu_2 + e_2 \end{array}\right\} \tag{3.19}$$

The error term, e_1, is normally distributed with a mean of zero and a standard deviation of s_1. The second error term, e_2, is also normally distributed with a mean of zero. The standard deviation of the distribution of the second error term is s_2.

The null hypothesis is that no substantive change has occurred. The theoretical interpretation of the null hypothesis in terms of true scores is that the true scores are equal ($\mu_1 = \mu_2$, or $\mu_1 - \mu_2 = 0$). Applying the null hypothesis, we obtain the following equation between the observed score difference and the difference between error components:

$$\begin{aligned} z_2 - z_1 &= (\mu_2 - \mu_1) + (e_2 - e_1) \\ \\ &= 0 + (e_2 - e_1) \\ \\ &= e_2 - e_1 \end{aligned} \tag{3.20}$$

Therefore, the difference between the observed scores is normally distributed with a mean of zero and a variance of $s_1^2 + s_2^2$ when true scores are identical. A test statistic, ξ, equal to a weighted difference score and defined by Equation 3.21, is normally distributed with a mean of zero and a variance of 1.0 when true scores are identical:

$$\xi = (z_2 - z_1)/(s_1^2 + s_2^2)^{\frac{1}{2}} \tag{3.21}$$

If ξ is greater than 1.96, the null hypothesis is rejected and it is inferred that a substantively meaningful nonzero difference between true scores exists. If ξ is less than 1.96, the null hypothesis is not rejected and it is inferred that no significant nonzero true score difference exists.

The mathematical details concerning the assessment of the significance of change for individuals have been described above. The purpose of these procedures is to determine if an observed score difference for the same individual corresponds to a meaningful true score difference or is merely due to chance. The remainder of this section will be devoted to the presentation of three examples of the application of the procedure described above. One example will be concerned with a case where a significant increase in true score has occurred. The first example is a case where the null hypothesis is rejected and meaningful gains in true scores exist. The second example concerns a case where the observed score difference does not correspond to a significant change in true scores. The second example is a case where the null hypothesis is accepted and meaningful (nonzero) true score differences do not exist. The third example is a case where a significant decrease in true scores has occurred.

Assessing the Significance of Individual Score Gains

When a particular student is administered a test at two points in time and the student's score obtained from the second administration is greater than the score obtained from the first administration, two questions arise: (1) Does the gain in observed scores indicate that a significant positive change or gain has occurred? (2) Is the observed score difference an artifact of measurement error or due to chance and not indicative of a meaningful positive true score change? The purpose of this section is to present two examples of the test of the significance of observed score increases. The first example concerns a case where a meaningful gain is evident. The second example concerns a case where meaningful gain has not occurred.

True Score Gain

In the fall of the school year, a student enrolled in an algebra class was administered a test designed to assess symbol manipulation skills. An equivalent test was administered in the spring of the same school year. The Rasch test scores assigned to the student are shown in Table 3.6. In this school, entrance into the next mathematics course in the sequence is based, in part, upon the recommendation of the teacher. The student's teacher felt that it was necessary to

TABLE 3.6

Rasch Test Scores for a Particular Student Obtained
from a Test of Algebraic Symbol Manipulation Administered in the Fall and Spring of the School Year

Test Administration	Test Score	Standard Error
Fall	-0.25 (z_1)	0.15 (s_1)
Spring	0.75 (z_2)	0.20 (s_2)

Source: Compiled by the author.

determine whether or not meaningful learning had occurred with
respect to symbol manipulation before the teacher could recommend
the student for promotion.

The null hypothesis is that there is no change in true scores
between the two administrations ($\mu_{fall} = \mu_{spring}$). The test scores and
their associated standard errors were substituted into Equation 3.21
to determine the value of the test statistic, ξ. The details of that
calculation follow:

$$\xi = \frac{z_2 - z_1}{\sqrt{s_1^2 + s_2^2}} = \frac{.75 - (-.25)}{\sqrt{(.15)^2 + (.20)^2}}$$

$$= \frac{.75 + .25}{\sqrt{.0225 + .040}} = \frac{1.00}{\sqrt{.0625}} \tag{3.22}$$

$$= \frac{1.00}{.25} = 4.00$$

Because the value of the test statistic ($\xi = 4.00$) is greater than
the critical value of the normal deviate at the 95 percent confidence
level (1.96), the null hypothesis ($\mu_{fall} = \mu_{spring}$) was rejected. The
student's teacher was 95 percent confident that a meaningful increase
in true score occurred. Alternatively, test scores with a difference
this large ($\xi = 4.00$) correspond to a meaningful true score gain 95
times out of 100. Equipped with the test information and other data
the teacher gathered throughout the school year, the student was
recommended for promotion to the next mathematics course.

Nonsignificant Gains

It is possible for a student to be administered a test on two different occasions in which the score assigned by the test on the second administration is greater than the score assigned at the first administration, and no meaningful true score difference exists. This occurs when the observed scores are different ($z_1 \neq z_2$), but that difference is not sufficiently large enough to infer that any true score difference ($\mu_1 - \mu_2 \neq 0$) exists. The purpose of this part is to present an example of such a situation.

A particular student is enrolled in a remedial English composition course at a junior college. The student received this distinction by obtaining a score on a preliminary screening examination that was below a cutoff score established by the faculty. The college policy is that any student must repeat a particular unit until significant gains are evidenced by pretest and posttest results. The pretest and posttest scores obtained by this particular student are shown in Table 3.7. The instructor's dilemma is to determine whether or not the observed score difference implies a true score difference. If the observed score difference corresponds to a significant true score gain, the student must go on to the next instructional unit in the sequence. If the observed score difference does not imply a meaningful true score gain, the student must be issued another instructional unit related to the unit the student was assigned previously.

The value of the normal deviate, ξ, corresponding to the observed score difference is calculated by substituting the test results into Equation 3.21. The observed score difference is $z_2 - z_1 = -.75 - (-1.25) = 0.50$. The standard error of this difference is

$$\sqrt{(.60)^2 + (.45)^2} = \sqrt{.36 + .2025} = \sqrt{.5625} = .75$$

TABLE 3.7

Pretest and Posttest Results of a Particular Student Obtained from a Test of Sentence Structure Competence

Test Administration	Test Score	Standard Error
Pretest	-1.25 (z_1)	$.60$ (s_1)
Posttest	$-.75$ (z_2)	$.45$ (s_2)

Source: Compiled by the author.

The value of the appropriate test statistic, ξ, is the quotient of the observed score difference and the standard error of that difference ($\xi = .50/.75 = .667$). As the value of the test statistic is less than the value of the normal deviate at the 95 percent significance level (1.96), the inference is that no meaningful true score gains have occurred. The instructor assigned the student to an alternative unit concerning sentence structure.

Assessing the Significance of Negative Change

When a test is administered to a particular student on two different administrations and the second test score is less than the first, two questions are often asked: (1) Has the student become confused in the intervening period between testing and is not as operationally function after the second testing as he/she was at the first testing? (2) Is the observed score difference due to measurement error and not indicative of a meaningful true score decrease? The purpose of this section is to present an example of situations reflected by these questions and the application of the significance testing model to this problem. The first example relates to the situation where a true score decrease has occurred. The second example concerns the situation where an observed score decrease does not correspond to a meaningful true score decrease.

Significant True Score Decrease

A particular student was involved in an instructional experiment. The student was also involved in two treatments. The treatments were sequential in the sense that the student experienced the second treatment after completing the first. A test was administered after the student completed each treatment. The reader familiar with experimental design will recognize this situation as a repeated measurement design. The test scores obtained by this particular student are shown in Table 3.8. The question posed is whether or not the observed score difference is meaningful in terms of a true score decrease.

The significance of the true score difference corresponding to the observed score difference can be assessed using Equation 3.21. The absolute value of the difference score is $|-.25 - .75| = |-1.00| = 1.00$. The standard error of the difference is

$$\sqrt{(.40)^2 + (.20)^2} = \sqrt{.16 + .04} = \sqrt{.20} = .447$$

The value of the test statistic, ξ, is the quotient of the absolute difference and the standard error of that difference ($\xi = 1.00/0.447 = 2.236$).

TABLE 3.8

Rasch Test Scores Obtained by a Particular Individual
After Each of Two Treatments

Treatment	Test Score	Standard Error
1	.75 (z_1)	.40 (s_1)
2	-.25 (z_2)	.20 (s_2)

Source: Compiled by the author.

Because the observed value of the test statistic is greater than the
critical value (1.96) at the 95 percent significance level, it is concluded that, for this particular student, the true scores have decreased.
The second treatment has been detrimental in some way to the student.

No Significant Decrease

A second student was subjected to the same repeated measurement scheme described above. The test results assigned to this
particular individual are shown in Table 3.9. The major issue with
these data is identical to the issue discussed above. Do the data support the hypothesis that the treatments exhibit a significant differential
effect on this particular individual?

The significance of the observed score change can be assessed
using the data in Table 3.9 and Equation 3.21. The absolute value of
the score difference is $|1.25 - 1.50| = |-.25| = .25$. The standard
error of the difference is the square root of the sum of the squares of
the standard errors corresponding to each test score:

$$\sqrt{(1.00)^2 + (.80)^2} = \sqrt{1.00 + .64} = \sqrt{1.64} = 1.281$$

TABLE 3.9

Test Results for an Individual Involved
in a Repeated Measurement Design

Treatment	Test Score	Standard Error
1	1.50 (z_1)	1.00 (s_1)
2	1.25 (z_2)	.80 (s_2)

Source: Compiled by the author.

The value of the test statistic is the quotient of the absolute difference and the standard error of that difference ($\xi = .25/1.281 = .195$). Because the value of the test statistic is less than the critical value (1.96), it is concluded that no true score difference is reflected in the data. The data do not support a differential treatment effect for this particular individual.

The mathematical model for assessing the significance of change scores has been presented in this section. In addition, examples of the application of the model to score gains as well as score decreases have been presented. The remaining section of this chapter will describe procedures for making ratio-level judgments concerning Rasch scores and assessing the significance of measurement differences between individuals.

COMPARISON OF RASCH MEASUREMENTS
BETWEEN INDIVIDUALS

The previous section of this chapter described a procedure for determining whether or not seemingly different test scores for the same individual are reflective of different true scores. If it is found that two test scores are reflective of different true scores, substantive meaning is often imparted to that difference. It would be useful to express the scores in terms of a ratio scale. For example, after a treatment a student exhibited twice or three times the ability level that the student exhibited before treatment. In addition, it is often desirable to compare the scores of two people on a ratio scale. For example, John Doe has two or three times the ability or attainment level of another student Sally Smith.

It was pointed out in the previous chapter that most of the discussion will surround logarithmic Rasch measurements. The logarithmic scale is an interval scale in the sense that the substantive meaning associated with the distance between any two particular adjacent points on the scale is identical to that meaning associated with the distance between any two other adjacent points on the same scale. The interval scaling property is convenient in that many arithmetic operations can be performed with numbers obtained from such scales (Guilford 1954). Unfortunately, one of the arithmetic operations that cannot be performed is multiplication. As division of ratios and multiplication are one and the same, scores obtained using logarithmic scales cannot be compared in ratio. The purpose of this section is to describe a procedure by which ratio judgments can be made. There are two subsections: The first subsection describes the mathematical model for making comparisons in terms of ratios, and the second presents some examples of the applications of that model.

Intraindividual Significance Testing

This subsection describes a mathematical model for comparing test scores obtained by two individuals. Consider two individuals who were administered the same or equivalent Rasch tests. The score assigned to one individual by the test is symbolized by z_1 and the associated standard error by s_1. The Rasch measurement assigned to the second individual is symbolized by z_2 and the associated standard error by s_2. If the symbols e_1 and e_2 are used to symbolize the error scores and the symbols μ_1 and μ_2 correspond to the true scores for the respective individuals, the fundamental measurement model implies that a strict relationship exists between observed and true scores and the error components. These relationships are defined by the following equations:

$$\left. \begin{array}{l} z_1 = \mu_1 + e_1 \\[2mm] z_2 = \mu_2 + e_2 \end{array} \right\} \tag{3.23}$$

The error scores are assumed to be normally distributed with a mean of zero and a standard deviation equal to the standard error or measurement.

By subtraction, the two equations result in a single equation relating the difference in observed scores $(z_2 - z_1)$, the true score difference $(\mu_2 - \mu_1)$, and the error score difference $(e_2 - e_1)$.

$$z_2 - z_1 = (\mu_2 - \mu_1) + (e_2 - e_1) \tag{3.24}$$

The purpose of this model is to determine if an observed score difference $(z_2 - z_1 \neq 0)$ is reflective of a significant true score difference $(\mu_2 - \mu_1 \neq 0)$. The null hypothesis is that there is no difference in true scores $(\mu_2 - \mu_1 = 0)$. Under the null hypothesis, the difference between observed scores is due to error alone.

$$H0: \quad z_2 - z_1 = e_2 - e_1 \tag{3.25}$$

Because the error score e_1 is normally distributed with a mean of zero and a variance of s_1^2 and the second error component, e_2, is similarly distributed with a mean of zero and a variance of s_2^2, the observed score difference is normally distributed with a mean of zero and a variance of $s_1^2 + s_2^2$. Consider the test statistic, ξ, defined by the following equation:

$$\xi = \frac{z_2 - z_1}{\sqrt{s_1^2 + s_2^2}} \tag{3.26}$$

Because the observed score difference, $z_2 - z_1$, is normally distributed with zero mean and known variance, the test statistic, ξ, is similarly distributed with zero mean and unit variance.

The significance of the difference between two observed scores can be determined by calculating the value of the test statistic, ξ, and comparing the critical value of the standard normal deviate at the desired significance level with the value of the test statistic. At the 95 percent significance level, if the value of the test statistic is greater than 1.96, it can be inferred that a significant difference in true scores exists. If the value of the test statistic is less than the critical value, no real true score difference is implied by the data at the 95 percent confidence level.

Ratio Comparisons

It was previously stated that logarithmic Rasch measurement scales are not ratio scales. That is, the ratio of two logarithmic scores for the same individual on two different tests or occasions or the ratio of logarithmic scores assigned to two individuals by a particular test or equivalent tests is not psychometrically meaningful. There is a transformation of the logarithmic scores that will result in a ratio scale. If x is a logarithmic scale score, then the quantity e^x, or, equivalently, exp(x), defines a ratio scale of Rasch logistic test scores (Wright 1967; Wright and Panchapakesan 1969; Kifer, Mattson, and Carlid 1975; Rasch 1966). The constant, e, is called the natural base of logarithms and is numerically equal to 2.718+.

The scale resulting from the exponential transformation of a logarithmic scale will be called the exponential scale. Scores obtained from the exponential scale will be called exponential scale scores. If z is a logarithmic scale score and Z is the corresponding exponential scale score, the two scores are related by the equation $Z = \exp(z)$ or $z = \text{Ln}(Z)$.

Consider the logarithmic scale scores z_1 and z_2 obtained by a particular individual on two equivalent tests or the same test administered on two different occasions. The procedures for determining the significance of true score differences described previously in this chapter are performed, and it is found that true score differences exist ($\mu_2 \neq \mu_1$). It is desired to know in terms of a ratio the amount of change that has occurred. Without loss of generality, assume that z_2 is greater than z_1. The procedure for determining the ratio-level comparison involves the transformation of the logarithmic scores z_1 and z_2 to the exponential scores Z_1 and Z_2 and computing the ratio of the exponential scores. The reader familiar with the exponential function will recognize that this result is numerically equivalent to the result obtained by allowing the exponential function to operate on the difference between the two logarithmic scores $(Z_2/Z_1 = \exp(z_2 - z_1))$. If the symbol ρ is used to symbolize the logistic ratio scale comparison, then the following equation defines the relation between the ratio of the exponential scale scores and the logarithmic scale scores:

$$\rho = \frac{z_2}{z_1} = \frac{\exp(z_2)}{\exp(z_1)} = \exp(z_2 - z_1) \qquad (3.27)$$

The procedure can be applied directly to the ratio-level comparison of scores obtained by two different individuals obtained using the same test or equivalent tests.

Let z_1 and z_2 correspond to the logarithmic scale scores assigned to two persons, respectively. If it has been found that the two scores reflect different true scores, then a ratio-level comparison can be made. Again, without loss of generality, assume that z_2 is greater than z_1. The ratio-level comparison can be obtained by direct substitution into Equation 3.27.

The mathematical details concerning a model for comparing test scores obtained by two individuals and for making ratio-level comparisons has been presented. The remainder of this chapter will present two examples of the application of the model. The first example concerns the calculation of the ratio-level comparison between test scores obtained by a particular individual using a particular test administered on two different occasions. The second example concerns the calculation of a ratio level comparison of the scores obtained by two different individuals obtained from the same test.

Examples of Ratio-Level Comparisons

In the previous section an example was presented in which a particular student was administered a test of symbol manipulation ability in the fall and spring of the school year. The logarithmic and exponential test scores are shown in Table 3.10. The exponential test score was obtained as the exponential function of the logarithmic test score $(Z_1 = \exp(z_1) = \exp(-.25) = .779$ and $Z_2 = \exp(z_2) = \exp(.75) = 2.117)$.

The ratio of the two exponential scale scores (Z_2/Z_1) results in a ratio-level estimate of the seasonal difference:

$$\rho = Z_2/Z_1 = 2.117/0.779 = 2.717 \qquad (3.28)$$

The result indicates that not only did the student increase in attainment $(\mu_2 > \mu_1)$ but also that the student's attainment increased by a factor

TABLE 3.10

Logarithmic and Exponential Rasch Test Scores
for a Particular Individual in the Fall and Spring
of the School Year

Test Administration	Logarithmic Score	Exponential Score
Fall	-.25(.15)	.779
Spring	.75(.20)	2.117

Note: Standard errors are enclosed in parentheses.
Source: Compiled by the author.

of 2.7, or approximately three times the attainment level reflected in the fall.

Consider two individuals (called individuals 1 and 2) who were each administered the same test. The scores assigned to each individual by the test are shown in Table 3.11. It is desired to determine the ratio of the abilities of these two individuals. The process for determining the ratio of the abilities of these two individuals is twofold. First, it must be determined if the test scores reflect a true score difference between the individuals. Second, if a significant true score difference is indicated, the ratio of the exponential scale scores is calculated.

The difference between observed logarithmic scale scores is 1.05 and the standard error of this difference is

$$\sqrt{(.50)^2 + (.10)^2} = \sqrt{.25 + .01} = \sqrt{.26} = .509$$

TABLE 3.11

Logarithmic and Exponential Test Scores
for Two Individuals.

Individual	Logarithmic Score	Standard Error	Exponential Score
1	-1.30	.50	.273
2	- .25	.10	.779

Source: Compiled by the author.

The value of the test statistic, ξ, given these values of the difference score and the standard error of the difference score, is the ratio of the difference score and the standard error of that difference: $1.05/0.509$, or 2.059. Because the value of the test statistic is greater than the critical value of 1.96, it is concluded that the observed scores reflect significantly different true scores. If no significant true score difference is detected, it would not make any sense to calculate a ratio, as this ratio would be 1.0. Because the difference was found to be significantly different from zero, it is not a waste to calculate a ratio of the two scores. The ratio of the exponential test scores is $.779/.273$, or 2.853. The inference is that the test scores indicate that one student reflects approximately three times the ability of the other student.

This chapter has presented procedures by which the Rasch test scores obtained by individuals can be interpreted and compared. The comparison procedures concerned the assessment of true score differences for test scores obtained by two different individuals from the same or equivalent tests. In addition, procedures for making ratio-level comparisons when true score differences exist have been presented. A general model of Rasch measurements has also been presented and applied to each of the inferential problems. The last chapter of this volume will describe procedures by which Rasch test scores can be used for the purposes of program and treatment evaluation. The general measurement model described in this chapter will be extended in the next chapter to the problem of program evaluation and the assessment of treatment differences.

4

TREATMENT AND PROGRAM
EVALUATION MODELS

The use of Rasch test scores for the assessment of individual ability and attainment has been discussed in previous chapters. Tests are commonly used for another purpose. Tests of ability or attainment are often used for the purpose of educational and social program evaluation as well as criteria in designed experiments. The purpose of this chapter is to present procedures by which Rasch tests can be used for the purpose of program evaluation and as criteria in many experimental designs.

The particular designs considered in this chapter are two-group comparisons, pretest versus posttest treatment versus control contrasts, repeated measurement designs with k replications, and factorial designs with k levels. Although each design is described in this chapter, no attempt at rigorous design descriptions is attempted. The purpose of this chapter is to describe procedures by which the fundamental measurement model can be applied to each design. The reader interested in the details concerning each design is referred to the experimental design literature (Blalock 1964; Campbell and Stanley 1963; Kerlinger 1973; Winer 1971). Examples of the application of the theory to each design are presented. In certain instances matrix algebra and vector notation were necessary to specify the model and equations effectively. The reader interested in presentations of matrix and vector procedures is referred to the many excellent presentations in the literature (Bock 1975; Finn 1974; Kerlinger and Pedhazer 1973; Rummel 1970).

This chapter contains six major sections. The first section extends the fundamental measurement model developed in the previous chapter to groups of individuals. The second section describes procedures by which the fundamental measurement model can be used for making inferences between two groups of individuals. The next section considers the application of the fundamental measurement model to situations where two groups of individuals are defined (treatment and control), a test was administered at the start of the experiment (pretest) or program, and the same test or an equivalent test was administered at the end of the program or after the treatment was administered to one of the two groups (posttest). The fourth section is concerned with the same group of subjects who have been subjected to two or more programs or treatments. The fifth section describes the application of the fundamental measurement model to the situation where two or more groups of individuals are compared with respect to their group or aggregate mean test score with respect to the same criterion or instrument. The sixth section presents examples of the application of the measurement model to higher-order factorial designs.

EXTENSION OF THE FUNDAMENTAL MEASUREMENT MODEL TO AGGREGATIONS OF INDIVIDUALS

In the previous chapter a relation between the observed test score, z, for a particular individual, the true score, μ, for that individual and an error component, e, was defined. A true score was defined as a test score for which the error of measurement was exactly zero (that is, a measurement without error). The observed score was defined as the sum of the true score and an error term ($z = \mu + e$). The definition of an observed score in terms of a true score and an error term was called the fundamental measurement model. The model further specified that the error term, e, was normally distributed with a mean of zero and a standard deviation equal to the standard error of measurement associated with the observed score, s. The purpose of this section is to extend the results obtained using the fundamental measurement model with individual test scores to test scores, or more accurately, aggregated test scores, obtained from groups of individuals.

Consider a group of N subjects. The observed test score for the ith individual is symbolized by z_i. The true score and error components for the ith subject are symbolized by μ_i and e_i, respectively. The error component is distributed as $\mathcal{N}(0, s_i^2)$, where s_i symbolizes the standard error associated with the Rasch test score, z_i, obtained by the ith individual. Using this notation, the fundamental measurement model implies a specific functional relation between the three quantities z_i, μ_i, and e_i. That functional relation is defined by Equation 4.1:

$$z_i = \mu_i + e_i \tag{4.1}$$

where

$$e_i \sim \mathcal{N}(0, s_i^2)$$

Define the mean or average score for the group, $\bar{Z}$, as the sum of the observed scores for each of the individuals composing the group (sum over all i, i = 1, ..., N) divided by the number of subjects in the group (N). Equation 4.1 can be used to determine the relation between the group mean, the individual true scores, and the individual error scores.

$$\bar{Z} = \frac{1}{N} \sum_{i=1}^{N} \mu_i + \frac{1}{N} \sum_{i=1}^{N} e_i \tag{4.2}$$

Define the mean true score for the group, $\bar{\mu}$, and the mean error component for the group, $\bar{e}$, as the average of the true scores and error components over all individuals composing the group. The mean true score, $\bar{\mu}$, is a single parameter characteristic of the group in the space of true scores or error-free measurements. The mean observed score, $\bar{Z}$, is an estimate of the mean true score. That estimate contains error (the estimate is not error-free). Equation 4.2 can be rewritten in terms of the mean true score and the mean error component.

$$\bar{Z} = \bar{\mu} + \bar{e} \tag{4.3}$$

To specify completely the model depicted by Equation 4.3, it is necessary to determine the distribution of the mean error term. If it is assumed that the error terms e_i and e_j ($i \neq j$) are stochastically independent, the distribution of $\bar{e}$ can be completely specified.

Assume that the individuals who compose the group are independent stochastically. Stochastic independence means that the responses, or equivalently the test scores, of any one particular individual are not necessarily dependent upon the test score or item responses of any other individual or group of individuals. The fundamental measurement model stipulates that each error term, e_i, is normally distributed with a mean of zero and known variance, s_i^2. A well-known result of probability theory states that if N stochastically independent random variables, x_i, are distributed as $\mathcal{N}(M, s_i^2)$, then the mean of the random variables is distributed as $\mathcal{N}(M, S^2)$ where S^2 is the mean of the individual variances, s_i^2 (Harris 1966; Freund 1962). Therefore, the mean error term, $\bar{e}$, is normally distributed with a mean of zero and a standard deviation equal to the square root of the mean of the squares of the individual standard errors.

It is now possible to specify a corollary to the fundamental measurement model. If a group consists of N subjects, the observed, true, and error components associated with the ith individual are symbolized by z_i, μ_i, and e_i, respectively, the observed scores are stochastically independent, and $\bar{Z}$, $\bar{\mu}$, and $\bar{e}$ symbolize the mean observed, true score, and error components, respectively, then the mean scores are related by the following equation:

$$\bar{Z} = \bar{\mu} + \bar{e} \tag{4.4}$$

where

$$\bar{e} \sim \mathcal{N}(0, S^2)$$

and

$$S^2 = \frac{1}{N} \sum_{i=1}^{N} S_i^2$$

This corollary will be called the fundamental measurement model for groups.

A measurement model specifying the relationship between the mean observed, true score, and error components for any particular group has been presented. It has been demonstrated that the group model is a direct extension of the fundamental measurement model presented in previous chapters. The remainder of this chapter will be concerned with applying this group model to two-group comparisons, pretest versus posttest and treatment versus control group designs, repeated measurement designs, as well as factorial comparisons.

BETWEEN-GROUP COMPARISONS

In many situations the investigator is concerned with comparing two groups of subjects with respect to some criterion. The investigator may randomly assign subjects to one of two groups. One of the groups receives some treatment while the other group does not receive the treatment. An evaluator may be interested in the differences (if any) in achievement exhibited by two groups of students, each group having used one of two texts. Two comparable groups are selected. One group uses one of the two texts while the second group uses the other text. The evaluator compares the two groups with respect to two achievement tests. The purpose of this section is to present the procedure by which the fundamental measurement model can be applied to this problem.

Consider two groups, group 1 and group 2. Group 1 contains $N(1)$ subjects and the second group contains $N(2)$ members. The Rasch test score, true score, error component, and standard error for the ith individual in the jth group (j = 1 or 2 in this case) are symbolized by z_{ij}, μ_{ij}, e_{ij}, and s_{ij}, respectively. The mean observed score, true score, and error components for the jth group are symbolized by $z_{.j}$, $\mu_{.j}$ and $e_{.j}$, respectively. The standard error of measurement corresponding to the group mean, $z_{.j}$, of the jth group will be symbolized by $s_{.j}$. The global group parameters can be written in terms of the components of the observed score for each individual composing the respective groups by using the fundamental measurement model for groups presented in the previous section.

$$z_{.j} = \frac{1}{N(j)} \sum_{i=1}^{N(j)} z_{ij} \tag{4.5}$$

$$z_{.j} = \mu_{.j} + e_{.j} \tag{4.6}$$

where

$$e_{.j} \sim N(0, s^2_{.j})$$

and

$$s^2_{.j} = \frac{1}{N(j)} \sum_{i=1}^{N(j)} s^2_{ij} \tag{4.7}$$

Consider two groups of individuals. The following relations can be written directly from Equations 4.6 and 4.7.

$$\left. \begin{aligned} z_{.1} &= \mu_{.1} + e_{.1} \\ z_{.2} &= \mu_{.2} + e_{.2} \end{aligned} \right\} \tag{4.8}$$

where

$$e_{.1} \sim N(0, s^2_{.1}), \quad e_{.2} \sim N(0, s^2_{.2})$$

and

$$s^2_{.1} = \frac{1}{N(1)} \sum_{i=1}^{N(1)} s^2_{i1}$$

$$s^2_{.2} = \frac{1}{N(2)} \sum_{i=1}^{N(2)} s^2_{i2}$$

Assume that the group means are not numerically identical ($z_{.1} \neq z_{.2}$). The issue of immediate concern is whether or not the nonzero difference of the group means ($z_{.1} - z_{.2} \neq 0$) implies a significant nonzero difference in true scores ($\mu_{.1} - \mu_{.2} \neq 0$). If the hypothesis $\mu_{.1} - \mu_{.2} = 0$ is accepted, the observed difference between the group means is due to measurement error. If the alternative hypothesis $\mu_{.1} - \mu_{.2} \neq 0$ is accepted, then the observed nonzero difference in group means is indicative of a substantively meaningful difference between groups. These hypotheses are specified below in terms of group true scores:

(Null Hypothesis) $\qquad$ H0: $\mu_{.1} - \mu_{.2} = 0$

(Alternate Hypothesis) $\qquad$ H1: $\mu_{.1} - \mu_{.2} \neq 0$

Using Equation 4.8 the observed mean difference, $z_{.1} - z_{.2}$, can be expressed in terms of a mean true score difference and a mean difference between error components.

$$z_{.1} - z_{.2} = (\mu_{.1} - \mu_{.2}) + (e_{.1} - e_{.2}) \qquad (4.9)$$

If the null hypothesis is true ($\mu_{.1} - \mu_{.2} = 0$), the observed score difference can be attributed entirely to measurement error.

$$z_{.1} - z_{12} = e_{.1} - e_{.2} \qquad (4.10)$$

Consider the test statistic, ξ, defined by the following equation:

$$\xi = \frac{z_{.1} - z_{.2}}{\sqrt{s^2_{.1} + s^2_{.2}}} \qquad (4.11)$$

Because $e_{.1}$ and $e_{.2}$ are normally distributed with a mean of zero and standard deviations of $s_{.1}$ and $s_{.2}$, respectively, the test statistic, ξ, is distributed as $N(0,1)$ if H0 is correct. Therefore, if ξ is greater than 1.96 (at the 95 percent significance level) the null hypothesis is rejected. If ξ is less than 1.96, the null hypothesis is accepted at the 95 percent significance level. If the test statistic is less than 1.96, the null hypothesis is accepted with 95 percent confidence and the difference between group means (if any) is attributed to measurement error. If the test statistic is greater than 1.96, the null hypothesis is rejected with 95 percent confidence and the nonzero difference between group means is attributed to a significant difference between true score means ($\mu_{.1} \neq \mu_{.2}$).

An Example of Two-Group Contrasts

A moderately sized suburban school system wishes to make a decision relative to the adoption of two possible textbooks. Initially, sufficient numbers of each textbook were purchased so that each book could be assigned to one and only one section. Students are alphabetically assigned to sections. The school officials felt that the groups of students were comparable. One group (designated as Textbook 1) had 10 students and the second group (designated as Textbook 2) had 12 students. A test designed to assess the competence of students relative to course objectives was administered to each group at the end of a trial period. The results of the testing are shown in Table 4.1.

The mean test score for the first group, $z_{.1}$, was .8749 ($s_{.1}$ = .5058). The mean test score for the second group, $z_{.2}$, was -.5057 ($s_{.2}$ = .3991). The difference between group means ($z_{.1} - z_{.2}$) was .8749 - (-.5057) = .8749 + .5057, or 1.3806. The observed difference between group means was clearly nonzero. The standard error of the difference in group means was

$$\sqrt{(.5058)^2 + (.3991)^2} = \sqrt{.2558 + .1593} = \sqrt{.4151}, \text{ or } .6443$$

The test statistic, ξ, defined by Equation 4.11 is the quotient of the difference between group means (1.3806) and the standard error of that difference (.6443). Therefore, the value of the test statistic, ξ, is 1.3806/.6443, or 2.1428. Because the value of the test statistic is greater than the critical value of a unit normal deviate at the 95 percent significant level (1.96), the null hypothesis was rejected. These results indicate that there is a true score difference between group means, and the textbooks seem to have a differential impact upon students. In so much as one can ascertain that no difference other than the textbook used existed between groups, the textbook designated as textbook 1 is the better book.

The procedure for comparing two groups of individuals administered the same or equivalent instruments has been presented. An example of the application of that procedure has also been described. The remainder of this chapter will describe the application of the fundamental measurement model to treatment versus control and pretest versus posttest, repeated measures, and factorial designs.

TABLE 4.1

Exemplary Test Results from an Evaluation of Two Different Textbooks

| | Experimental Group | | | |
| | Textbook 1 | | Textbook 2 | |
	Test Score	Standard Error	Test Score	Standard Error
Individual measurements	1.828	.338	-4.417	.525
	-1.271	.281	2.078	.360
	5.417	.581	-1.037	.255
	-4.459	.527	.518	.180
	-3.407	.461	5.259	.573
	7.709	.694	-7.629	.691
	-3.097	.439	-3.815	.488
	-3.889	.493	1.907	.345
	5.034	.561	-.954	.244
	4.884	.552	-.477	.173
	—	—	2.380	.386
	—	—	.119	.086
Group mean	.8749	.5058	-.5057	.3991

Source: Compiled by the author.

69

TWO-GROUP PRETEST-POSTTEST EVALUATION DESIGNS

A classical experimental and evaluation design is the treatment control, pretest-posttest design. With this type of design two groups of subjects are selected. One group is administered an experimental treatment. The remaining group is not administered the treatment. The group that is administered the treatment is called the treatment or experimental group. The group that is not administered the treatment is designated as the control or reference group. A measurement (such as an ability or attainment test) relative to experimental or program criteria is obtained prior to administering the treatment to the experimental group. Pretreatment measurements (call the pretest) are obtained from each member of both groups (treatment and control). The same instrument or an equivalent instrument is used to obtain measurements after the treatment has been administered. The instrument used to obtain the posttreatment data is called the posttest. Posttest data are also obtained from each member of both groups (treatment and control).

The major inferential question relative to this type of design is whether or not the observed difference over time (posttest minus pretest) for the treatment group members is attributable to the treatment, to maturation, to the effect of being exposed to the pretest, or to some other nontreatment related phenomenon. The issue is addressed by comparing the difference over time for the treatment group with the difference over time for the nontreatment or control group. The question posed is whether or not the observed pretest-posttest difference observed for the treatment group is different from the same difference over time for the control group. If the differences over time for the two groups are not significantly different, it is concluded that the treatment did not have an effect upon the subjects. If the differences over time for the two groups are significantly different, it is concluded that the treatment did have an effect on the experimental subjects.

With this type of design there are two test scores for each individual (a pretest and a posttest score). Associated with each test score is a true score, error term, and a standard error of measurement. In order to simplify the notation a particular notational scheme has been employed (see Table 4.2).

The fundamental measurement model for group means results in four equations defining the relations between observed scores, true scores, and error components:

$$\bar{z}_{11} = \bar{\mu}_{11} + \bar{e}_{11} \tag{4.12}$$

$$\bar{z}_{12} = \bar{\mu}_{12} + \bar{e}_{12} \tag{4.13}$$

TABLE 4.2

Notational Scheme for Symbols Corresponding to Aggregated Data
for the Pretest Posttest Treatment Versus Control Group Design

| | Group Designation | | | |
| | Treatment | | Control | |
Index	Pretest	Posttest	Pretest	Posttest
Observed score	$\bar{z}_{11}$	$\bar{z}_{12}$	$\bar{z}_{21}$	$\bar{z}_{22}$
Standard error	$\bar{s}_{11}$	$\bar{s}_{12}$	$\bar{s}_{21}$	$\bar{s}_{22}$
Mean true score	$\bar{\mu}_{11}$	$\bar{\mu}_{12}$	$\bar{\mu}_{21}$	$\bar{\mu}_{22}$
Mean error term	$\bar{e}_{11}$	$\bar{e}_{12}$	$\bar{e}_{21}$	$\bar{e}_{22}$

Source: Compiled by the author.

$$\bar{z}_{21} = \bar{\mu}_{21} + \bar{e}_{21} \tag{4.14}$$

$$\bar{z}_{22} = \bar{\mu}_{22} + \bar{e}_{22} \tag{4.15}$$

where

$$\bar{e}_{11} \sim \mathcal{N}(0, \bar{s}_{11}^2); \ \bar{e}_{12} \sim \mathcal{N}(0, \bar{s}_{12}^2); \ \bar{e}_{21} \sim \mathcal{N}(0, \bar{s}_{21}^2)$$

and

$$\bar{e}_{22} \sim \mathcal{N}(0, \bar{s}_{22}^2)$$

The pretest-posttest difference (variation over time) for the
treatment group, Δ_t, and the control group, Δ_c, can be expressed in
terms of true scores and error terms. The expression of these differences is obtained by subtraction from Equations 4.12 to 4.15. These
differences are

$$\Delta_t = \bar{z}_{12} - \bar{z}_{11} = (\bar{\mu}_{12} - \bar{\mu}_{11}) + (\bar{e}_{12} - \bar{e}_{11}) \tag{4.16}$$

$$\Delta_c = \bar{z}_{22} - \bar{z}_{21} = (\bar{\mu}_{22} - \bar{\mu}_{21}) + (\bar{e}_{22} - \bar{e}_{21}) \tag{4.17}$$

Assume that the observed score mean differences for each group over
time are not equal ($\Delta_t - \Delta_c \neq 0$). The inferential question is whether
or not this nonzero difference ($\Delta_t - \Delta_c \neq 0$) implies a differential variation in the true scores over time (H1: $\bar{\mu}_{12} - \bar{\mu}_{11} \neq \bar{\mu}_{22} - \bar{\mu}_{21}$) or is

attributable to measurement error. The null hypothesis is that the observed nonzero difference $(\Delta_t - \Delta_c \neq 0)$ is due to measurement error and does not imply a significant differential variation in true scores (H0: $\bar{\mu}_{12} - \bar{\mu}_{11} \neq \bar{\mu}_{22} - \bar{\mu}_{21}$).

The difference between observed variations over time $(\Delta_t - \Delta_c)$ can be shown to be functionally related to the differential differences between true scores $([\bar{\mu}_{22} - \bar{\mu}_{21}] - [\bar{\mu}_{12} - \bar{\mu}_{11}])$ and an error term by subtracting Equation 4.16 from Equation 4.17. That functional relation is

$$\Delta_c - \Delta_t = (\bar{z}_{22} - \bar{z}_{21}) - (\bar{z}_{12} - \bar{z}_{11})$$

$$= [(\bar{\mu}_{22} - \bar{\mu}_{21}) - (\bar{\mu}_{12} - \bar{\mu}_{11})] + (\bar{e}_{22} - \bar{e}_{21} + \bar{e}_{11} - \bar{e}_{12}) \tag{4.18}$$

The standard error, S, of the differential contrast, $\Delta_c - \Delta_t$, is easily determined from the standard errors of the individual error terms.

$$S^2 = \bar{S}_{11}^2 + \bar{S}_{12}^2 + \bar{S}_{21}^2 + \bar{S}_{22}^2 \tag{4.19}$$

Assuming that the null hypothesis is true $[(\bar{\mu}_{22} - \bar{\mu}_{21}) - (\bar{\mu}_{12} - \bar{\mu}_{11})] = 0$, Equation 4.18 can be rewritten with only error components on the right side.

$$\Delta_c - \Delta_t = (\bar{z}_{22} - \bar{z}_{21}) - (\bar{z}_{12} - \bar{z}_{11})$$

$$= \bar{e}_{22} - \bar{e}_{21} + \bar{e}_{11} - \bar{e}_{12} \tag{4.20}$$

Equation 4.20 is a restatement of the null hypothesis that the nonzero value of the differential contrast, $\Delta_c - \Delta_t$, was entirely attributable to measurement error. The standard error of the differential contrast is expressed by Equation 4.19.

Consider the test statistic, ξ, defined b the quotient of the values of the differential contrast, $\Delta_c - \Delta_t$, and the associated standard error, S.

$$\xi = \frac{\Delta_c - \Delta_t}{S}$$

$$\tag{4.21}$$

$$= \frac{(\bar{z}_{22} - \bar{z}_{21}) - (\bar{z}_{12} - \bar{z}_{11})}{\sqrt{\bar{s}_{11}^2 + \bar{s}_{12}^2 + \bar{s}_{21}^2 + \bar{s}_{22}^2}}$$

The values of the test statistic, ξ, are normally distributed with a mean of zero and a variance of 1.0. Therefore, if the value of the test statistic is greater than the expected value of the normal deviate (1.96 at the 95 percent significance level), the null hypothesis is rejected. If the null hypothesis is rejected, it is inferred that a differential variation in true scores exists and the treatment had some effect on the subjects in the treatment group that was not evident in the control group. If the value of the test statistic is less than the expected value of the normal deviate, the null hypothesis is not rejected. If the null hypothesis is not rejected, it is inferred that a differential variation in true scores over time is not evident in the data and the treatment did not exhibit any effect upon the subjects in the treatment group that was not also evident in the control group.

At this point a theoretical discussion of the use of the fundamental measurement model for group data relative to making inferences regarding the pretest-posttest, treatment-control design has been presented. The following example describes the numerical details necessary to apply the model.

Example of the Pretest-Posttest Two-Group Design

A school district considered adopting an individualized instructional sequence in general mathematics. An issue that concerned the teacher union officials and the district supervisors was whether the increased learning (if any) experienced by students taught individually over students traditionally taught would warrant the expenditure of teacher time. It had not been demonstrated that any difference existed at all between the individualized and traditional instructional modes. It was decided to conduct an experiment. Four hundred students were randomly assigned to one of two treatment groups. One group with 200 students was to be taught using the individualized instructional mode (the treatment group). The remaining 200 students were to be taught traditionally (the control group). Each of the two groups consisted of 10 classrooms, and teachers were randomly assigned to classrooms. Each student was administered a comprehensive general mathematics test at the beginning and at the end of the school year. The results of the testing are shown in Table 4.3.

The average pretest and posttest scores for the subjects assigned to the treatment group were 2.735 and 5.707, respectively. The average pretest and posttest scores for the subjects assigned to the control group were 2.031 and 4.755, respectively. Therefore, the score difference, Δ_t, for the treatment group subjects over time was 5.707 - 2.735, or 2.972. The test score difference, Δ_c, for the subjects assigned to the control group was 5.744 - 2.031, or 2.724. The value of the differential contrast, $\Delta_c - \Delta_t$, is 2.724 - 2.972, or .248 in absolute value. The standard error of the differential contrast is

TABLE 4.3

Aggregate Group Data from a Pretest-Posttest Experimental Design

Experimental Group	Instrument				Number of Subjects
	Pretest		Posttest		
	Mean	Standard Error	Mean	Standard Error	
Treatment	2.735	.413	5.707	.597	200
Control	2.031	.356	4.755	.545	200

Source: Compiled by the author.

equal to the square root of the sum of the squares of the standard errors of each group.

$$S = \sqrt{(.413)^2 + (.356)^2 + (.597)^2 + (.545)^2} = \sqrt{.951} = .975$$

The value of the test statistic, ξ, defined by Equation 4.21 is the quotient of the values of the differential contrast and the standard error to the differential contrast. Therefore, the value of the test statistic is .248/.975, or .254. This value of the test statistic is not greater than the critical value of a unit normal deviate at the 95 percent significance level (1.96). It is inferred that no differential variation in true scores was observed for this data set. Therefore, no significant improvement was observed for subjects assigned to individualized general mathematics programs that was not also observed for traditionally instructed students.

A procedure for the application of the fundamental measurement model to pretest-posttest experimental designs has been presented in this section. An example of the application of the procedure to such a design has also been presented. The remainder of this chapter will discuss procedures for using Rasch measurements and the fundamental measurement model for repeated measurement and factorial designs. The next section of this chapter is concerned with the repeated measurement design. The final section will be concerned with the k group factorial design.

REPEATED MEASUREMENT DESIGNS WITH k REPLICATIONS

Consider a set of k possible treatments. A group of N subjects are exposed to each of the k treatments. Therefore, there exist k test scores for each of the N individuals. Such a design is called a repeated measurement design with k replications.

The jth test score for the ith individual, z_{ij}, is considered to be the sum of the true score for that individual, μ_i, a constant component due to the presence of the treatment, t_j, and an error factor, e_{ij}. The standard error of the jth measurement for the ith individual is symbolized by s_{ij}. The observed score for the ith individual obtained during the jth treatment is considered to be an estimate of the sum of the true score component due to the treatment. The observed score for a particular individual is conceptualized as the sum of the individual's true score, a true score component for the treatment, and an error component.

$$z_{ij} = \mu_i + t_j + e_{ij} \tag{4.22}$$

where

$$e_{ij} \sim \mathcal{N}(0, s_{ij}^2)$$

The experimenter is often concerned with whether or not treatment p results in scores that are different from the scores obtained for the same subjects in treatment q (that is, $t_p = t_q$ or $t_p \neq t_q$). The null hypothesis in this case is that there is no between-treatment effect and $t_p = t_q$. Consider the difference between the scores obtained for the same individual when involved with each of the treatments, $z_{ip} - z_{iq}$.

$$
\begin{aligned}
z_{ip} - z_{iq} &= (\mu_i + t_p + e_{ip}) - (\mu_i + t_q + e_{iq}) \\
&= (t_p - t_q) + (e_{ip} - e_{iq})
\end{aligned} \tag{4.23}
$$

Under the influence of the null hypothesis, the difference between treatment true scores is exactly zero, $t_p - t_q = 0$. Therefore, the observed score difference can be expressed in terms of random error.

$$z_{ip} - z_{iq} = e_{ip} - e_{iq} \tag{4.24}$$

Because the distributions of the error terms are known, it is also known that the distribution of the variable, ξ_i, defined by Equation 4.25, is normal with zero mean and unit variance.

$$\xi_i = \frac{z_{ip} - z_{iq}}{\sqrt{s_{ip}^2 + s_{iq}^2}} \tag{4.25}$$

Because ξ_i is distributed as $N(0,1)$, the sum of the squares of the ξ_i over each of the N subjects is distributed as chi-square with N degrees of freedom (Harris 1966; Freund 1962). Define the test statistic ξ_{pq} corresponding to a contrast between treatments p and q by Equation 4.26. If ξ_{pq} is greater than the critical value of the chi-square statistic with N degrees of freedom, the null hypothesis is rejected and it is inferred that a significant between-treatment effect exists. If the value of ξ_{pq} is less than the critical value of chi-square, the null hypothesis is not rejected and it is inferred that no significant treatment effect exists.

$$\xi_{pq} = \sum_{i=1}^{N} \xi_i^2 = \sum_{i=1}^{N} \frac{(z_{ip} - z_{iq})^2}{s_{ip}^2 + s_{iq}^2} \tag{4.26}$$

The model developed in this section can be extended to multigroup contrasts. The set of all test scores for the ith individual can be considered to form a matrix, Z_i, with k columns. The set of all standard errors can be considered to form a matrix, S, with N rows and k columns. The standard errors for a particular subject form a particular row of the S matrix. The multigroup contrast can be written in terms of a $1 \times k$ row vector, Δ. The elements of the row vector, Δ, sum to zero ($\Sigma_{i=1}^{k} \Delta_i = 0$) and correspond to the contrast of interest.

For example, in an experiment with three replications the contrast vector, Δ, contains three elements (a 1×3 matrix). If one wished to contrast the first treatment with the second treatment, the required contrast vector would be $(1,-1,0)$. If one wished to contrast the second treatment with the mean of the first and third treatments, the required contrast vector would be $(-\frac{1}{2}, 1, -\frac{1}{2})$. An argument similar to that presented for the two-group repeated measurement case results in the observation that the test statistic defined by Equation 4.27 is distributed as chi-square with N degrees of freedom.

$$\xi_\Delta = \sum_{i=1}^{N} \frac{(\Delta Z_i^T)^2}{S_i^2} \tag{4.27}$$

where

$$S_i^2 = \sum_{j=1}^{k} \Delta_j^2 s_{ij}^2$$

Test statistics for making inferential statements relative to treatment contrasts in the k treatment repeated measurement model

TABLE 4.4

Test Results for a Hypothetical Repeated Measurement Design

Student	Discipline		
	Harsh	Moderate	Lax
1	1.32 (.27)	1.67 (.41)	.82 (.15)
2	2.71 (.62)	3.51 (.65)	1.21 (.16)
3	1.41 (.20)	2.60 (.60)	.51 (.10)
4	3.56 (.65)	4.80 (.70)	2.61 (.60)
5	.85 (.15)	2.30 (.55)	1.30 (.17)

Note: Standard errors are enclosed in parentheses.
Source: Compiled by the author.

have been presented. The remainder of this section will present an example of the application of the model.

An experimenter wished to determine whether or not the amount of discipline reflected in the climate of a classroom affected the achievement of students in that classroom. In this hypothetical experiment five students were subjected to three experimentally manipulated discipline conditions: harsh, moderate, and lax. A general achievement test was administered after each treatment. The test results are shown in Table 4.4.

The experimenter hypothesized that the observed difference between moderate and lax discipline groups was significant. The data were presented for analysis in the form shown in Table 4.5. The value of the chi-square test statistic for this contrast was 36.062 with five degrees of freedom. The probability of obtaining a value of chi-square at least this large due to chance was less than .001. The experimenter concluded that the data indicated that students educated in moderately disciplined environments tended to achieve more than students in classrooms that lacked discipline.

The experimenter also wished to contrast the subjects who were enrolled in harshly disciplined classrooms with those enrolled in moderately disciplined or lax classrooms. This was a multitreatment comparison. The required contrast vector was $\Delta = (1, -\frac{1}{2}, -\frac{1}{2})$. The test score, Z, and standard error, S, matrices are shown below.

TABLE 4.5

Arrangement of Data for a Two-Group
Repeated Measurement Contrast

Student	Test Results Discipline Treatment		$z_{12} - z_{13}$	$s_{12}^2 + s_{13}^2$	ξ_1^2
	Moderate	Lax			
1	1.67 (.41)	.82 (.15)	.85	.191	3.791
2	3.51 (.65)	1.21 (.16)	2.30	.448	11.805
3	2.60 (.60)	.51 (.10)	2.09	.370	11.806
4	4.80 (.70)	2.61 (.60)	2.19	.850	5.642
5	2.30 (.55)	1.30 (.17)	1.00	.331	3.018

Note: Standard errors are enclosed in parentheses.
Source: Compiled by the author.

$$Z = \begin{bmatrix} 1.32 & 1.67 & .82 \\ 2.71 & 3.51 & 1.21 \\ 1.41 & 2.60 & .51 \\ 3.56 & 4.80 & 2.61 \\ .85 & 2.30 & 1.30 \end{bmatrix} \quad S = \begin{bmatrix} .27 & .41 & .15 \\ .62 & .65 & .16 \\ .20 & .60 & .10 \\ .65 & .70 & .60 \\ .15 & .55 & .17 \end{bmatrix}$$

The values of the matrices ΔZ^T and $\Delta(S^2)^T$ were determined by
matrix multiplication and are shown below.

$$\Delta Z^T = \begin{bmatrix} .075 \\ .350 \\ -.145 \\ -.145 \\ -.950 \end{bmatrix} \quad \Delta(S^2)^T = \begin{bmatrix} .121 \\ .496 \\ .133 \\ .635 \\ .105 \end{bmatrix}$$

The value of the test statistic is the quotient of the square of
the ith entry in the ΔZ^T matrix and the ith entry in the $\Delta(S^2)^T$ matrix
summed over all subjects

$$\xi_\Delta = \frac{(.075)^2}{.121} + \frac{(.350)^2}{.496} + \frac{(-.145)^2}{.133} + \frac{(-.145)^2}{.635} + \frac{(-.950)^2}{.105}$$

This value of the test statistic was not greater than the critical value of chi-square with five degrees of freedom at the .05 level (11.07). It was concluded that no significant difference existed between subjects who were subjected to harsh discipline when compared to both moderate and lax discipline treatments.

FACTORIAL MEASUREMENT DESIGNS

At this juncture the analysis of data obtained from two different groups of individuals or the same group of individuals exposed to different treatments has been discussed. The behavioral researcher often uses another type of design, which concerns the comparison of more than two groups with respect to the same attribute. For example, the achievements of five groups of students are compared where each group of students had been exposed to a particular type of instruction. This type of design is called a factorial design with k levels. The number of levels is equal to the number of groups. For the example cited, k equals 5. The purpose of this section is to discuss the treatment of the factorial design with k levels.

For the purposes of this presentation, assume that there are k groups, wht number of subjects in the jth group is symbolized by $n(j)$, and the total number of subjects is symbolized by N. The observed score and standard error for the ith subject in the jth group will be symbolized by z_{ij} and s_{ij}, respectively. The average observed score and the group standard error for all subjects regardless of group assignment will be symbolized by $z_{..}$ and $s_{..}$. The aggregate group mean and standard errors can be computed using the following equations:

$$z_{..} = \frac{1}{N} \sum_{j=1}^{k} \sum_{i=1}^{n(j)} z_{ij} \tag{4.28}$$

$$s_{..}^2 = \frac{1}{N} \sum_{j=1}^{k} \sum_{i=1}^{n(j)} s_{ij}^2 \tag{4.29}$$

Three major questions arise concerning the factorial design. First, does there exist significant variation between individuals? That is, do individuals vary significantly from the grand mean? If a significant variation between individuals and the grand mean is not found, further analysis would be useless. Second, do the groups as aggregates in themselves vary significantly from the grand mean? If the group means are not significantly different from the grand mean, then the analysis of specific contrasts would not be useful. Third, do particular groups differ significantly from other groups? Are the first two groups different from the third in a three-factorial design? Is textbook A different from all other textbóoks? These are the questions the analysis procedures presented in this section address.

Variation Between Individuals

The major issue to be addressed in this section is whether or not an observed variation between the measurements obtained for each individual and the grand mean implies that the true scores for the individuals are also significantly different from the true score corresponding to the grand mean. Consider the test score, z_{ij}, true score, μ_{ij}, and error term, e_{ij} corresponding to individual i in group j. In addition, consider the true score, $\mu_{..}$, and error component, e corresponding to the grand mean. Using the fundamental measurement model, the following equations can be written between observed scores, true scores, and error components:

$$\left. \begin{array}{l} z_{ij} = \mu_{ij} + e_{ij} \\ z_{..} = \mu_{..} + e_{..} \end{array} \right\} \tag{4.30}$$

where

$$e_{ij} \sim \mathcal{N}(0, s_{ij}^2) \quad \text{and} \quad e_{..} \sim \mathcal{N}(0, s_{..}^2)$$

The deviation between the observed score for each individual and the observed mean score can be written, given Equation 4.30, in terms of a true score difference and an error term.

$$z_{ij} - z_{..} = (\mu_{ij} - \mu_{..}) + (e_{ij} - e_{..}) \tag{4.31}$$

Under the null hypothesis, true scores for individuals and the group mean true score are not different ($\mu_{ij} - \mu_{..} = 0$). Therefore, if the null hypothesis is to be accepted, the deviation between observed scores and the grand mean must be attributable to error. Consider the index, d_{ij}, defined by Equation 4.32:

$$d_{ij} = \frac{z_{ij} - z_{..}}{(s^2_{ij} + s^2_{..})^{\frac{1}{2}}}$$

(4.32)

$$= \frac{e_{ij} - e_{..}}{(s^2_{ij} + s^2_{..})^{\frac{1}{2}}}$$

If the null hypothesis is to be accepted, then the deviation statistic, d_{ij}, defined above, is normally distributed with zero mean and unit variance. Given the deviation statistic for a particular individual (that is, a particular set of values for i and j), the significance of the deviation of that particular individual's measurement from the grand mean can be determined by consulting a table of probabilities for the unit normal deviate.

The assessment of the significance of departures from the grand mean for each individual is very laborious. However, a global statistic summarizing the deviations for all individuals can be easily obtained. Because the individual deviation statistics, d_{ij}, are distributed as $N(0,1)$ if the null hypothesis is accepted, the sum of the squares of these deviations is distributed as chi-square with N degrees of freedom. This is true because the sum of the squares of random variables that are sampled from a unit normal population is distributed as chi-square (Harris 1966; Freund 1962). Therefore, if we define the test statistic, ξ_{total}, as a measure of the overall variation of individual true scores from the grand mean true score, that statistic is distributed as chi-square with N degrees of freedom.

$$\xi_{total} = \sum_{j=1}^{k} \sum_{i=1}^{n(j)} \frac{(z_{ij} - z_{..})^2}{s^2_{ij} + s^2_{..}}$$

(4.33)

If the test statistic, ξ_{total}, defined by Equation 4.33 is less than the critical value of the chi-square statistic (df = N), significant individual variation exists and further analysis is suggested.

Variation Between Groups

A global statistic by which the significance of the true score variation from the grand mean can be assessed has been presented. Once true score variation at the individual level has been determined, one can turn attention to the level of the group. The question of interest here is whether or not the observed variations between observed group mean scores and the observed grand mean are sufficient to imply that the group mean true scores are significantly different from the grand mean true score. If the true scores of the groups are not significantly different from the grand mean true score, the analysis of variations between particular sets of groups is not justified. If the true scores corresponding to at least one group is significantly different from the true score corresponding to the grand mean, then examination of particular contrasts is justified. The purpose of this section is to describe a procedure by which this issue can be addressed.

Consider the mean of the measurements obtained over all subjects who belong to the jth group, $z_{.j}$, and the standard error of that mean, $s_{.j}$. If stochastic independence is assumed, the group mean and standard error can be found using the fundamental measurement model for grouped data.

$$z_{.j} = \frac{1}{n(j)} \sum_{i=1}^{n(j)} z_{ij} \qquad (4.34)$$

$$s^2_{.j} = \frac{1}{n(j)} \sum_{i=1}^{n(j)} s^2_{ij} \qquad (4.35)$$

The fundamental measurement model for groups can be easily applied to these data and an equation relating the observed group mean, $z_{.j}$, with the group mean true score, $\mu_{.j}$, and error component, $e_{.j}$, results. That equation is

$$z_{.j} = \mu_{.j} + e_{.j} \qquad (4.36)$$

$$z_{..} = \mu_{..} + e_{..} \qquad (4.37)$$

where

$$e \sim \mathcal{N}(0, s^2_{.j}) \text{ and } e_{..} \sim \mathcal{N}(0, s^2_{..})$$

If Equation 4.37 is subtracted from Equation 4.36, the observed difference between the group mean and the grand mean can be expressed in terms of the true score difference and an error term:

$$z_{.j} - z_{..} = (\mu_{.j} - \mu_{..}) + (e_{.j} - e_{..}) \qquad (4.38)$$

If the null hypothesis is to be accepted, the group mean and grand mean true scores should not be significantly different ($\mu_{.j} - \mu_{..} = 0$). Therefore, the observed difference between group and grand mean should be distributed as a normal deviate with a mean of zero and a variance equal to $s^2_{.j} + s^2_{..}$. The weighted deviation, $d'_{.j}$, should be distributed as a centralized unit normal deviate.

$$d'_{.j} = \frac{z_{.j} - z_{..}}{(s^2_{.j} + s^2_{..})^{\frac{1}{2}}} \tag{4.39}$$

The weighted deviation score, $d'_{.j}$, indicates a technique for determining the deviation of particular group means from the grand mean. If the observed value of the weighted deviate is greater than 1.96 (at the 95 percent significance level), it can be concluded with 95 percent confidence that the true group mean score is significantly different from the grand mean true score. If the observed value of the weighted deviate, $d'_{.j}$, is less than 1.96, it can be concluded that the group mean true score is not significantly different from the grand mean true score at the 95 percent confidence level. Of course, any desired confidence level can be applied for significance testing.

In addition to testing each group for departure from the grand mean, a global statistic for making inferences about the set of all groups is available. Because the weighted deviation statistic, $d'_{.j}$, is distributed as a unit normal deviate, the sum of the squared values of the deviation statistics summed over all groups (values of j) is distributed as chi-square with k degrees of freedom.

$$\xi_{b.groups} = \sum_{j=1}^{k} \frac{(z_{.j} - z_{..})^2}{s^2_{.j} - s^2_{..}} \tag{4.40}$$

If the value of the global statistic defined by Equation 4.40 is greater than the expected value of the chi-square statistic with k degrees of freedom at the desired significance level, it can be concluded that the group mean true scores depart significantly from the grand mean true score. If the value of the global statistic is less than the expected value of the chi-square statistic with k degrees of freedom at the desired significance level, the null hypothesis is accepted and it is concluded that the group mean true scores are not significantly different from the global mean true score.

Between-Group Contrasts

In addition to ascertaining the significance of the variation between individuals and globally between groups, it is often desired to assess the significance of the variation between the means of particular groups or sets of groups. Procedures by which the variation of particular groups or sets of groups are to be studied will be presented in this section. The procedure is, in practice, not very different from either the two-group or k-group repeated measurement problems discussed previously in this chapter.

Consider the situation where there exist k groups as described above. It is desired to contrast a particular set of group means with another particular set of group means. The contrast can be conveniently defined in terms of what are called contrast vectors. Contrast vectors have been discussed previously in this chapter. However, a brief review will be presented at this point.

Contrast Vectors

A contrast vector is a $1 \times k$ row vector with k columns (where k is the total number of groups). For the purposes of discussion, contrast vectors will be symbolized by ψ. Assume that there are three groups for a particular application (k = 3). To contrast the first group with the second group and not consider the third group, the appropriate contrast vector would be $(1,-1,0)$ To contrast the mean of the first two groups (considered as a conglomerate or as one group) with the third group, the appropriate contrast would be $(\frac{1}{2},\frac{1}{2},-1)$. Each contrast can be associated with a particular aggregated mean equal to the sum of the group means weighted by the appropriate entry in the contrast vector. For example, if the means of groups 1, 2, and 3 are 1.25, 6.41, and 2.86, respectively, the value, z_ψ, of the contrast vector $\psi = (\frac{1}{2},\frac{1}{2},-1)$ would be $\frac{1}{2}(1.25) + \frac{1}{2}(6.41) + (-1)(2.86)$, or 0.97. The standard error of a contrast value, s_ψ, is equal to the square root of the sum of the squares of the standard errors of the group means weighted by the square of the appropriate entry in the contrast vector squared. For example, if the standard errors of the means of three groups are .20, 2.16, and .56, respectively, the standard error of the contrast value for the contrast $\psi = (\frac{1}{2},\frac{1}{2},-1)$ would be the square root of $(\frac{1}{2})^2(.20)^2 + (\frac{1}{2})^2(2.16)^2 + (-1)^2(.56)^2 = 1.490$, or 1.221.

If the jth entry of a contrast vector, ψ, is symbolized by ψ_j, the value of the contrasted means and the standard error of that value are expressed by the following equations:

$$z_\psi = \sum_{j=1}^{k} z_{.j}\psi_j \qquad (4.41)$$

$$s_\psi^2 = \sum_{j=1}^{k} s_{.j}^2\psi_j^2 \qquad (4.42)$$

If the value of a contrast is not significantly different from zero, it is concluded that the mean of the two sets of groups that compose the contrast (are contrasted) are not significantly different from each other. If the value of a contrast is significantly different from zero, it is concluded that the mean of the two sets of contrasted groups are significantly different. The remainder of this section will be concerned with the problem of assessing the significance of the departure of the observed value of the contrast from zero.

Using the fundamental measurement model for groups, the value of a contrast can be expressed in terms of contrasted group true scores and an error term. That expression is shown by the following equation:

$$z_\psi = \mu_\psi + e \tag{4.43}$$

where

$$\mu_\psi = \sum_{j=1}^{k} \psi_j \mu_{.j} \quad \text{and} \quad e_\psi = \sum_{j=1}^{k} \psi_j e_{.j}$$

The null hypothesis for this problem is that there is no significant difference between groups and that the true score value of the contrasted group mean true scores is zero ($\mu_\psi = 0$). If the null hypothesis is accepted, the observed value of the contrasted group means, z_ψ, is due to error ($z_\psi = e_\psi$). Therefore, the value of the weighted value of the contrast defined by the statistic, ξ_ψ, and Equation 4.44 is distributed as a centralized unit normal deviate:

$$\xi_\psi = \frac{z_\psi}{s_\psi} = \frac{\displaystyle\sum_{j=1}^{k} \psi_j z_{.j}}{\left(\displaystyle\sum_{j=1}^{k} \psi_j s_{.j}^2\right)^{\frac{1}{2}}} \tag{4.44}$$

If the $1 \times k$ matrix, Z, is the matrix of group means and S^2 is a $k \times k$ matrix such that the squared group standard errors are inserted on the diagonal and zeros elsewhere, Equation 4.44 can be written more succinctly in terms of matrix notation:

$$\xi_\psi = \frac{\psi Z^T}{(\psi S^2 \psi^T)^{\frac{1}{2}}} \tag{4.44a}$$

If the value of the test statistic, ξ_ψ, is less than 1.96, the groups represented by the contrast weights are not assumed to be significantly different at the appropriate significance level. If the value of the test statistic, ξ_ψ, is greater than 1.96, the groups represented by the contrast weights are assumed to be significantly different at the 95 percent significance level.

At this point the details of procedures for analyzing a factorial design using Rasch measurements have been presented. One issue concerned the assessment of whether observed variation between individuals constituted a significant departure from the grand mean. A second issue concerned whether or not observed variation between group means constituted a significant departure from the grand mean. The third issue concerned whether or not particular contrasts were indicative of significant differences between sets of groups. Examples of the application of these procedures will constitute the remainder of this chapter.

Another Discipline Experiment

An experimenter wished to investigate the relationship between classroom discipline and student achievement. Students were assigned to one of three groups. The groups were designated as traditional, mild, and lax. The students assigned to the traditional group received instruction from a teacher who was rated by her peers as being a strong disciplinarian. The students assigned to the mild or lax groups were taught by teachers who were rated as being mild or lax disciplinarians. Due to the movement of students between classes within the school, the number of students who remained with particular teachers was small. The results of the final achievement testing are shown in Table 4.6.

It appeared upon inspection of the test results that there was considerable variation between students and that the students assigned to the teacher who was a mild disciplinarian exhibited higher achievement levels than did students assigned to the other teachers. The hypothesis that there was significant variation between subjects was tested using the ξ_{total} test statistic described by Equation 4.34. The value of the ξ_{total} test statistic was found to be 85.7578 with 16 degrees of freedom. The probability of obtaining a value of chi-square as large as 85.7578 with 16 degrees of freedom is less than .001. The first null hypothesis that there is no significant variation between subjects was rejected. It was concluded that sufficient variation between subjects existed to warrant further analysis.

The value of the between-group chi-square was calculated using Equation 4.40. The values of the group deviations statistics were

TABLE 4.6

Hypothetical Test Scores for a Factorial Study
of Classroom Discipline

| | Experimental Group | | |
	Traditional	Mild	Lax
Individual data	1.080 (.259)	1.203 (.274)	.117 (.086)
	.119 (.086)	.062 (.062)	1.152 (.268)
	.000 (.080)	1.232 (.277)	.523 (.181)
	1.091 (.261)	.016 (.032)	.044 (.052)
	.067 (.065)	2.069 (.360)	
	1.081 (.260)		
	.045 (.053)		
Group mean	.498 (.179)	.916 (.239)	.459 (.169)
d_j'	.039	-.129	.039
Grand mean	.6189 (.1977)		
Total test statistic	85.7578 (df = 16)		
Between–group test statistic	1.4984 (df = 2)		

Note: Standard errors are enclosed in parentheses.
Source: Compiled by the author.

87

calculated using Equation 4.39. The setup of these calculations is shown below:

$$\xi_{b.groups} = \frac{(.498 - .619)^2}{(.179)^2 + (.198)^2} + \frac{(.916 - .619)^2}{(.239)^2 + (.198)^2} + \frac{(.459 - .619)^2}{(.169)^2 + (.198)^2}$$

$$= 1.4984 \tag{4.45}$$

$$d_1' = (.498 - .619)/\sqrt{(.179)^2 + (.198)^2} \tag{4.46}$$

$$d_2' = (.916 - .619)/\sqrt{(.239)^2 + (.198)^2} \tag{4.47}$$

$$d_3' = (.459 - .619)/\sqrt{(.169)^2 + (.198)^2} \tag{4.48}$$

Each of the individual group deviation statistics was less than the value of 1.96 expected for the normal deviate at the .95 level. In addition, the value of the between-group test statistic was 1.4984 with two degrees of freedom. The probability of obtaining a value of chi-square this large or larger due to chance was greater than 0.30. The second null hypothesis that the group means were not significantly different from the grand mean was accepted. The researcher concluded that although considerable variation existed between subjects the data (as limited as they were) did not indicate that the degree to which a classroom teacher was a disciplinarian had an effect upon student achievement.

A Textbook Selection Experiment

An evaluator was assigned the task of determining whether or not one of three possible textbooks had a differential impact upon student achievement. Three groups of students were selected. Each of the students in a particular group was instructed using a particular textbook. Teachers were randomly assigned to textbook groups. The results of an attainment test administered at the end of the school year were tabulated for each of the three groups. The results of that tabulation are shown in Table 4.7.

The null hypothesis that the students did not exhibit differential behavior was tested using the total chi-square statistic. That statistic was calculated using Equation 4.3. The value of the test statistic was 2218.05 (df = 477). The probability of obtaining a value of chi-square this large or larger is less than .01. The null hypothesis was rejected. It was concluded that significant variation between students existed and that further analysis was justified.

TABLE 4.7

Hypothetical Aggregate Data for a Factorial Evaluation of Textbooks

	Textbook Used		
Index Reported	Textbook A	Textbook B	Textbook C
Group mean	.654 (.068)	-.851 (.151)	-.364 (.046)
Number of subjects	273	136	68
Deviation statistics	4.845	-5.187	-4.136
Grand mean		.080 (.097)	
Total deviation statistic		2218.05 (df = 477)	
Between-group statistic		67.4934 (df = 2)	

Note: Standard errors are enclosed in parentheses.
Source: Compiled by the author.

The values of the between-group and deviation statistics were calculated using Equations 4.40 and 4.39. The setups for those calculations are shown below:

$$d_1' = (.654 - .080)/\sqrt{(.068)^2 + (.097)^2} = 4.845 \tag{4.49}$$

$$d_2' = (-.851 - .080)/\sqrt{(.151)^2 + (.097)^2} = -5.187 \tag{4.50}$$

$$d_3' = (-.364 - .080)/\sqrt{(.046)^2 + (.097)^2} = -4.136 \tag{4.51}$$

$$\xi_{b.groups} = (4.845)^2 + (-5.187)^2 + (-4.136)^2 = 67.4934 \tag{4.52}$$

The value of the between-group test statistic was 64.4934 with two degrees of freedom. The probability of obtaining a value of chi-square as large or larger due to chance was less than .001. The absolute value of each deviation statistic was greater than 1.96. The null hypothesis that no between-group variation existed was rejected. It was concluded that the group means deviated significantly from the grand mean and further analysis of these differences was indicated.

The department chairperson was concerned with differences that may exist between textbooks A and B and between the combination of A and B with textbook C. These concerns were translated into contrast vectors. The contrast vector corresponding to a test of the mean differences between books A and B is $\psi_1 = (1,-1,0)$. The contrast vector corresponding to the contrast of combination of groups A and B with group C is $\psi_2 = (\frac{1}{2},\frac{1}{2},-1)$. The values of the contrasts and their associated standard errors were calculated using Equations 4.41 and 4.42. The setups for each of those calculations are shown below:

$$z_{\psi_1} = (1)(.654) + (-1)(-.851) + (0)(-.364) = 1.505 \tag{4.53}$$

$$z_{\psi_2} = (\tfrac{1}{2})(.654) + \tfrac{1}{2}(-.851) + (-1)(-.364) = .2655 \tag{4.54}$$

$$s^2_{\psi_1} = (1)^2(.068)^2 + (-1)^2(.151)^2 + (0)^2(.046)^2 = .0274 \tag{4.55}$$

$$s^2_{\psi_2} = (\tfrac{1}{2})^2(.068)^2 + (\tfrac{1}{2})^2(.151)^2 + (-1)^2(.046)^2 = .008972 \tag{4.56}$$

The values of the normal deviates corresponding to each of the two contrasts were calculated using Equation 4.41. The value of the normal deviate corresponding to any particular contrast is equal to the value of that contrast divided by the standard error of that value. Examples of the setup of each calculation are shown below:

$$\psi_1 = \frac{1.505}{\sqrt{.02743}} = 9.0870 \tag{4.57}$$

$$\psi_2 = \frac{.2655}{\sqrt{.008972}} = 2.8029 \tag{4.58}$$

The values of each of the test statistics are greater than the critical value of 1.96 at the 95 percent level. It was concluded that students assigned textbook A exhibited markedly higher achievement than students assigned either of the other textbooks. Also, if a choice was to be made to purchase quantities of both textbooks A and B or to purchase only textbook C, then textbook C is the better choice—a lesser of two evils. The evaluators recommended that textbook A be adopted.

HIGHER-ORDER FACTORIAL DESIGNS

Many experimenters find themselves attempting to answer questions that cannot be written as a traditional one-way design. In many cases more than one factor is required to frame the hypothesis adequately. Using traditional instruments, the researcher may use a two- or higher-order factorial analysis of variance design. The purpose of this section is to describe how these higher-order factorial designs can be examined utilizing Rasch measurements. It will the seen that these higher-order designs do not require additional mathematical formulations. The equations generated in the previous sections are, with the aid of contrast vectors, sufficient to estimate all main effects and interactions. Three examples will be presented. They will begin with a rather simple 2 × 2 design and proceed to a somewhat more complex 2 × 3 design with interaction.

A 2 × 2 Design

A researcher was interested in evaluating the impact of public law 94-142 on handicapped children. Public law 94-142 requires, in part, that handicapped children be integrated with nonhandicapped children to the maximum extent possible. This researcher wished to investigate whether or not integration enhanced learning and whether the impact was different for male than female handicapped children. Ninety-five handicapped children were selected from a metropolitan high school. The parents of the children were asked to designate whether they wished to have their child assigned to an integrated or segregated classroom. The researcher realized the limitations that this type of assignment procedure imposed on the experimental design. However, the particular school system would not allow random assignment and would only allow one set of achievement tests to be administered. The results of the end of year testing are shown in Table 4.8.

TABLE 4.8

Hypothetical Aggregate Data for an Evaluation of Public Law 94-142

| Sex | Type of Treatment | | | |
| | Integrated | | Segregated | |
	Male	Female	Male	Female
Mean test score	1.34 (.40)	.40 (.15)	.50 (.20)	1.74 (.62)
Number of a	40	20	20	15
Grand mean		1.03 (.38)		

Note: Standard errors are shown in parentheses.
Source: Compiled by the author.

As indicated in Table 4.8 this type of design is not different from the one-way designs described previously. In fact, any N-factorial design can be described in terms of a one-way layout. The between-group deviation statistics were calculated using Equations 4.40 and 4.39. The setups for those calculations are shown below:

$$d_1' = (1.34 - 1.03)/\sqrt{(.4)^2 + (.38)^2} \quad = \quad .562 \tag{4.59}$$

$$d_2' = (\ .40 - 1.03)/\sqrt{(.25)^2 + (.38)^2} = -1.542 \tag{4.60}$$

$$d_3' = (\ .50 - 1.03)/\sqrt{(.2)^2 + (.38)^2} = -1.234 \tag{4.61}$$

$$d_4' = (1.74 - 1.03)/\sqrt{(.62)^2 + (.38)^2} = \quad .579 \tag{4.62}$$

$$\xi_{b.group} = (.562)^2 + (-1.542)^2 + (-1.234)^2 + (.579)^2$$

$$= 4.240 \quad df = 3$$

The value of the between-group test statistic was 4.240 with three degrees of freedom. The probability of obtaining a value of chi-square as large due to chance was greater than .10. This result was not surprising, as the absolute value of each deviation statistic was less than 1.96. This result tends to indicate that "main effects" were absent.

However, two deviation statistics (d_2' and d_3'), although not significant, were rather large. The researcher decided to test for the presence of a sex × treatment interaction. The symbolic contrast vector for that interaction was $\psi = (\frac{1}{2}, -\frac{1}{2}, -\frac{1}{2}, \frac{1}{2})$. The value of the contrast and associated standard error were calculated using Equations 4.41 and 4.42. The setups for these calculations are shown below:

$$z_\psi = \tfrac{1}{2}(1.34) - \tfrac{1}{2}(.40) - \tfrac{1}{2}(.50) + \tfrac{1}{2}(1.74) = 2.18 \tag{4.63}$$

$$s_\psi^2 = (\tfrac{1}{2})^2(.40)^2 + (-\tfrac{1}{2})^2(.15)^2 + (-\tfrac{1}{2})^2(.20)^2 + (\tfrac{1}{2})^2(.62)^2$$

$$= .152 \tag{4.64}$$

The value of the normal deviate corresponding to the contrast was calculated as the ratio of the value of the contrast and the associated standard error.

$$\psi_1 = 2.18/(.152)^{\frac{1}{2}} = 5.597 \tag{4.65}$$

The value of ψ_1 is greater than the critical value of 1.96 at the 95 percent level. It was concluded that a significant interaction was present.

Females tended to exhibit greater scores in segregated classes than in integrated classrooms. On the other hand, males tended to exhibit greater test scores in integrated classrooms. The researcher concluded that the evidence indicated that males should be integrated and females should be placed in segregated classrooms. The school board concluded that such a policy could be considered as sufficient evidence for sex discrimination and voted to integrate all handicapped students rather than face a possible violation of the equal opportunity act.

A 3 × 3 Design

A school system has implemented a sequence of computer-assisted instruction in mathematics. The program was funded under Title I and designed to assist learning disabled students. An external evaluator was contracted. The evaluator was requested to determine whether or not the amount of time a student spent working with the computer was related to achievement. In addition, the school committee was interested in knowing if students in particular grades exhibited greater achievement than students of other grade levels. Students were allowed to enter the program only if they exhibited achievement test scores within a very narrow range. Therefore, the students did not substantively differ with respect to entrance behavior. A posttest was administered after the program was operating for six months. The results are shown in Table 4.9.

The overall deviation test statistic, $\xi_{b.group}$, was calculated using Equation 4.40. The setup for that calculation is shown below:

$$\xi_{b.group} = (-4.66)^2 + (-3.33)^2 + (1.72)^2 + (-4.20)^2$$

$$+ (-.45)^2 + (3.72)^2 + (-.87)^2 + (5.56)^2 \qquad (4.66)$$

$$= 107.70 \quad df = 8$$

The probability of obtaining a value of chi-square at least as large as 107.70 with eight degrees of freedom due to chance is less than .001. Therefore, significant between-group variation was evidenced.

Two orthogonal contrasts represent the total variation between grades. These contrasts are $\psi_1 = (1, -\frac{1}{2}, -\frac{1}{2}, 1, -\frac{1}{2}, -\frac{1}{2}, 1, -\frac{1}{2}, -\frac{1}{2})$ and $\psi_2 = (0, -1, 1, 0, -1, 1, 0, -1, 1)$. The first contrast, ψ_1, compares sixth-grade students with upper classpersons. The second contrast, ψ_2, compares seventh-grade students with eighth-grade students.

Two orthogonal contrasts represent the total variation between categories of time on the computer. These contrasts are $\psi_3 = (-1, -1, -1, \frac{1}{2}, \frac{1}{2}, \frac{1}{2}, \frac{1}{2}, \frac{1}{2}, \frac{1}{2})$ and $\psi_4 = (0, 0, 0, -1, -1, -1, 1, 1, 1)$. The first contrast,

TABLE 4.9

Posttest Results for a Hypothetical Program Evaluation

	Hours of Computer Instruction								
	Less Than 1 Hr.			1-2 Hr.			Greater Than 2 Hr.		
Grade in school	6	7	8	6	7	8	6	7	8
Group mean	.4	.6	1.9	.5	1.3	2.6	.7	1.2	3.6
Standard error	.1	.15	.2	.1	.18	.25	.15	.16	.34
Number of cases	20	20	20	20	20	20	20	20	20
Deviation statistics	-4.66	-3.33	1.72	-4.20	-.45	3.72	-2.93	-.87	5.56
Grand mean	1.42								
Global standard error	.195								

Source: Compiled by the author.

TABLE 4.10

Values of Test Statistics for a Particular 3×3 Design

Contrast	Δz_{ψ}	s_{ψ}	ξ_{ψ}
ψ_1	-4.0	.342	-11.70
ψ_2	5.0	.546	- 9.16
ψ_3	-2.1	.374	5.48
ψ_4	1.1	.518	2.12

Source: Compiled by the author.

ψ_3, compares the students with less than one hour of instruction with other students with greater exposure to the computer. The second contrast, ψ_4, compares students who experienced one to two hours of instruction with students who received more than two hours of instruction.

The values of each of the contrasts, the associated standard errors, and deviation test statistics were calculated using Equations 4.41 and 4.42. The values of these statistics are shown in Table 4.10. Each of the test statistics, ξ_{ψ}, was greater in absolute value than the critical value of a normal deviate at the 95 percent confidence level (1.96). Therefore, significant variation was observed between grades and between time of instruction groups.

The evaluator reported that sixth-grade students did not experience as great a level of achievement as upper classpersons. Seventh-grade students exhibited lower levels of achievement than their eighth-grade counterparts. In addition, the evaluator reported that students with less than one hour of instruction did not exhibit achievement levels as high as students who received greater amounts of instruction with the computer. Students who received more than two hours of instruction exhibited greater achievement levels than their counterparts who received one to two hours of instruction.

The 2×3 Design

A researcher wished to study the utility of peer teaching for handicapped children, gifted children, and children with no particular special need. Peer teaching involves using fellow students to assist particular students within the classroom. Sixty handicapped, 60 gifted,

TABLE 4.11

Hypothetical Posttest Results for a Peer Teaching Experimental
for a Peer Teaching Experimental Design

Teaching Technique	Type of Student					
	Handicapped		No Special Need		Gifted	
	Nonpeer	Peer	Nonpeer	Peer	Nonpeer	Peer
Group mean	1.41	5.68	8.70	4.93	9.57	6.53
Standard error	.14	.62	.64	.55	.75	.63
Deviation statistic	-7.82	-.54	2.95	-1.50	3.60	.45
Grand mean	6.14					
Global standard error	.588					

Source: Compiled by the author.

and 60 students with no particular special need were randomly selected
from the population of a large metropolitan school district. Within
each group, 30 students were assigned to traditional classrooms and
30 students were assigned to classrooms where peer teaching was
frequently employed. The peer and nonpeer teaching groups did not
differ in achievement at the beginning of the school year. A posttest
was administered at the end of the school year. The posttest results
are shown in Table 4.11.

The variation of group means from the grand mean was assessed
using the $\xi_{b.group}$ statistic defined by Equation 4.40. The setup for
that calculation is shown below:

$$\xi_{b.group} = (-7.82)^2 + (-.54)^2 + (2.95)^2 + (-1.50^2$$

$$+ (3.60)^2 + (.45)^2 = 85.59 \quad df = 5 \qquad (4.67)$$

The probability of obtaining a value of chi-square with five degrees
of freedom at least as large as 85.59 by chance is less than .05. It
was concluded that significant variation existed between groups and
that further investigation was warranted.

One contrast, ψ_1, was necessary to represent the variation
between teaching styles. That contrast is $\psi_1 = (1,-1,1,-1,1,-1)$. This
contrast compares nonpeer teaching groups with peer teaching classrooms.

Two contrasts are required to represent the variation between
the various types of students. The two contrasts are $\psi_2 = (\frac{1}{2}, \frac{1}{2}, -1, -1,$

$\frac{1}{2}, \frac{1}{2})$ and $\psi_3 = (-\frac{1}{2}, -\frac{1}{2}, 0, 0, \frac{1}{2}, \frac{1}{2})$. The first contrast, ψ_2, compares non-special needs students with special needs students (handicapped and gifted). The second contrast, ψ_3, contrasts handicapped and gifted students.

Two contrasts were required to define the interaction terms. The symbolic contrast vectors are $\psi_4 = (\frac{1}{2}, -\frac{1}{2}, -\frac{1}{2}, \frac{1}{2}, 0, 0)$ and $\psi_5 = (-\frac{1}{2}, \frac{1}{2}, 0, 0, \frac{1}{2}, -\frac{1}{2})$. The first contrast represents the handicapped-nonspecial needs by treatment interaction. The second symbolic contrast vector represents the special needs by treatment interaction.

The values associated with each of the five symbolic contrast vectors, the standard error of those values, and the appropriate test statistics were calculated using Equations 4.41 and 4.42. The results of these calculations are shown in Table 4.12.

The test statistic, ξ_ψ, corresponding to the first contrast, ψ_1, was found to be less than the critical value of 1.96. It was concluded that across students no significant effect could be associated with the type of teaching style. It was found that the students with special needs did perform less well than nonspecial needs students. The latter result is probably due to pretreatment variation. An examination of the test statistic corresponding to the third contrast vector indicates that the gifted students performed better than the handicapped students. This result was not unexpected and can be attributed to pretreatment differences between groups.

An analysis of the interaction contrasts (ψ_4 and ψ_5) yields substantively interesting results. The values of both contrasts were found to be significant at the .05 level. Therefore, significant interactions were present in the data. From an examination of the average test scores for each group, it was found that handicapped students assigned to peer teaching environments exhibited larger achievement

TABLE 4.12

Analysis of Contrasts for a 2 × 3 Factorial Design

Contrast	Δz_ψ	s_ψ	ξ_ψ
ψ_1	2.54	1.44	1.76
ψ_2	-2.04	1.03	1.99
ψ_3	4.50	.58	7.72
ψ_4	-4.02	.53	-7.61
ψ_5	3.66	.58	6.26

Source: Compiled by the author.

levels than handicapped students assigned to traditional classrooms. However, both gifted and nonspecial needs children exhibited lower achievement scores when assigned to peer teaching environments than their counterparts assigned to traditional classrooms. The researcher concluded that the peer teaching strategies are beneficial for handicapped children, but peer teaching may be detrimental to nonhandicapped students.

SUMMARY

This chapter has presented the mathematical models of Rasch measurement scales as they apply to evaluation and experimental design. The application of the fundamental measurement model to groups of individuals has also been presented. In particular the model has been applied to the analysis of two-group, repeated measures, and factorial designs.

This volume was intended to present the details concerning the Rasch model and a comparison of that model with the traditional psychometric model in a way that would be useful to the practitioner. Details and procedures for making interval and ratio comparisons of Rasch measurements between individuals have been presented. The presentation of the procedures for making individual level comparisons was intended to be at the level of the practitioner. The models and procedures used for making decisions at the individual level were extended to the level of treatment and program evaluation as well as experimental design. It was intended that the transition from the individual to the group level would be as straightforward as possible. The procedures for using the models at the group level were intended to be read at the level of the professional program evaluator. Examples of the application of each procedure were presented at both the individual and evaluation levels. It was intended that these examples would present clear amplifications of the theory.

Once again, sections of this volume were prepared to be read at two levels. Certain sections were intended for use by the practitioner. Other sections were intended to be useful to the professional evaluator. It is hoped that the volume has achieved these two objectives. In addition, certain amounts of new theory have been presented. It is hoped that this theory has been presented in a fashion that was sufficiently clear and precise to allow others to contribute modifications, extensions, and elaborations.

BIBLIOGRAPHY

Ahmann, J. S. and Glock, M. D. 1967. Evaluating Pupil Growth. 3rd ed. Boston: Allyn & Bacon.

Airasian, P. W. and Madaus, G. F. 1976. "A Study of the Sensitivity of School and Program Effectiveness Measures." Report submitted to the Carnegie Corporation of New York.

Anderson, E. B. 1973. "A Goodness of Fit Test for the Rasch Model." Psychometrika 38: 123-39.

Anderson, J., Kearney, G. E., and Everett, A. V. 1968. "An Evaluation of Rasch's Structural Model for Test Items." British Journal of Mathematical and Statistical Psychology 231-38.

Arneklev, B., Gee, D., and Ingebo, G. 1976. "Optimum Range of Difficulty for Linking Items." Paper presented at the Annual Meeting of the American Educational Research Association, San Francisco, April.

Blalock, H. M. 1964. Causal Inferences in Nonexperimental Research. New York: Norton.

Block, N. J., and Dworkin, G., eds. 1976. The IQ Controversy. New York: Pantheon.

Bock, R. D. 1975. Multivariate Statistical Methods in Behavioral Research. New York: McGraw-Hill.

Boldt, R. F. 1972. "An Estimation Procedure for the Rasch Model allowing for Missing Data." Research Memorandum 72-5. Princeton, N.J.: Educational Testing Service.

Brink, N. E. 1972. "Rasch's Logistic Model vs. the Guttman Method." Educational and Psychological Measurement 32: 921-27.

Campbell, D. T., and Stanley, J. C. 1963. Experimental and Quasi-Experimental Designs for Research. Chicago: Rand McNally.

Carroll, J. B. 1974. "Problems in the Factor Analysis of Tests of Edumetric." American Psychologist, July: 512-18.

____. 1950. "Problems in the Factor Analysis of Tests of Varying Difficulty." American Psychologist 5: 319.

Carver, R. P. 1975. "The Coleman Report: Using Inappropriately Designed Achievement Tests." American Educational Research Journal, Winter 12: 77-86.

Cobean, N., Airasian, P., and Rakow, E. 1975. "A Comparison of Discriminant Analysis and Intraclass Correlation for Selecting Items Which Maximally Discriminate Between Groups." Paper presented at the annual meeting of the New England Educational Research Organization, Provincetown, Mass., May.

Conover, W. J. 1971. Practical Nonparametric Statistics. New York: Wiley.

Doherty, V. S., and Forster, F. 1976. "Can Rasch Scaled Scores Be Predicted from a Calibrated Item Pool?" Paper presented at the annual conference of the American Educational Research Association, San Francisco, April.

Ebel, R. L. 1954. "Procedures for the Analysis of Classroom Tests." Educational and Psychological Measurement 14: 352-64.

Edwards, Allen L. 1957. Techniques of Attitude Scale Construction. New York: Appleton-Century-Crofts.

Ferguson, George A. 1971. Statistical Analysis in Psychology and Education. 3rd ed. New York: McGraw-Hill.

Finn, J. D. 1974. A General Model for Multivariate Analysis. New York: Holt, Rinehart and Winston.

Forbes, D. W. 1976. "The Use of Rasch Logistic Scaling Procedures in the Development of Short Multi-Level Arithmetic Tests for Public School Measurement." Paper presented at the annual conference of the American Educational Research Association, San Francisco, April.

____, and Ingebo, G. S. 1975. "An Empirical Test of the Content Homogeneity Assumption Involved in Rasch Item Calibration." Paper presented at the annual conference of the American Educational Research Association, Washington, D.C., April.

Forster, F. 1976. "Sample Size and Stable Calibrations." Paper presented at the annual conference of the American Educational Research Association, San Francisco, April.

Freund, J. E. 1962. Mathematical Statistics. Englewood Cliffs, N.J.: Prentice-Hall.

Guilford, J. P. 1954. Psychometric Methods. 2nd ed. New York: McGraw-Hill.

Gulliksen, Harold. 1950. Theory of MENTAL TESTS. New York: Wiley.

Hambleton, R. K., and Cook, Linda. 1976. "Introduction to Latent Trait Models and Their Use in the Analysis of Educational Test Data." Paper presented at the annual meeting of the National Council on Measurement in Education, San Francisco.

Hambleton, R. K., and Traub, R. E. 1973. "Analysis of Empirical Data using Two Logistic Latent Trait Models." British Journal of Mathematical and Statistical Psychology 26: 195–211.

Harris, Bernard. 1966. Theory of Probability. Reading, Mass.: Addison-Wesley.

Harvey, T. J. 1975. "Some Thoughts on Norm-Referenced and Criterion-Referenced Measures." Research in Education, May 17: 79-86.

Hashway, R. M. 1974. "The Error Function." American Journal of Physics, January 63.

____. 1976. "Can Tests Which Maximally Discriminate Between Individuals Also Detect Treatment Differences?" Paper presented at the Symposium on Applications of Statistics, Wright State University, Dayton, Ohio, June 14-18.

____. 1977. "A Comparison of Tests Derived Using Rasch and Traditional Psychometric Paradigms." Ph.D. diss. Boston College, Chestnut Hill, Mass., April. Available from University Microfilms, Ann Arbor, Mich.

Heald, M. A. 1969. "Least Squares Made Easy." American Journal of Physics, June 37: 655-62.

Henryssen, S. 1971. "Gathering, Analyzing, and Using Data on Test Items." In Educational Measurement. 2nd ed. Robert L. Thorndike, ed. Washington, D. C.: American Council on Education, pp. 130-59.

Hollander, Myles, and Wolfe, D. A. 1973. Nonparametric Statistical Methods. New York: Wiley.

Hoyt, C. J. 1941. "Test Reliability Estimated by Analysis of Variance." Psychometrika 6: 153-60.

Ingebo, G. S. 1976. "Item Pool Linking Procedures." Paper presented at the annual convention of the American Educational Research Association, San Francisco, April.

Kendall, M. G. 1970. Rank Correlation Methods. 4th ed. London: Charles Griffin.

Kerlinger, Fred N. 1973. Foundations of Behavioral Research. New York: Holt, Rinehart and Winston.

_____, and Pedhazur, E. J. 1973. Multiple Regression in Behavioral Research. New York: Holt, Rinehart and Winston.

Kifer, E. W., Mattson, I., and Carlid, M. 1975. Item Analysis Using the Rasch Model. Sweden: Institute for the Study of International Problems in Education, Stockholm University, June.

Lord, F. M. 1952. "A Theory of Test Scores." Psychometric Monographs 7.

_____, and Novick, M. R. 1974. Statistical Theories of Mental Test Scores. 2nd ed. Reading, Mass.: Addison-Wesley.

Massey, F. J. 1951. "The Kolmogorov-Smirnov Test for Goodness of Fit." Journal of the American Statistical Association 51.

Matarazzo, J. D. 1972. Wechsler's Measurement and Appraisal of Adult Intelligence. 5th ed. Baltimore, M.D.: Williams and Wilkins.

McNemar, Q. 1962. Psychological Statistics. 3rd ed. New York: Wiley.

Mead, R. J. 1974. Evaluation of Instruction Using the Rasch Latent Trait Model." Chicago: University of Chicago, MESA, August (mimeo.).

Mead, Wright, and Ginther, Haberman. 1974. "Analysis of Fit of Data to the Rasch Latent Trait Model." Chicago: University of Chicago, MESA, October.

Nunnally, J. C. 1967. Psychometric Theory. New York: McGraw-Hill.

Rakow, E. A., Airasian, P. W., and Madaus, G. F. 1976. "Assessing School and Program Effectiveness: Estimating Hidden Teacher Effects." Paper presented at the annual meeting of the National Council on Measurement in Education, San Francisco, April.

____, ____, and ____. 1975. "A Comparison of Two Item Selection Techniques for Program Evaluation." Paper presented at the annual meeting of the National Council on Measurement in Education, Washington, D.C., April.

Rasch, G. 1966. "An Item Analysis Which Takes Individual Differences Into Account." British Journal of Mathematics and Statistical Psychology, May 19: 49-55.

Rummel, R. J. 1970. Applied Factor Analysis. Evanston, Ill.: Northwestern University Press.

Spearman, C. 1927. The Abilities of Man: Their Nature of Measurement. New York: Macmillan.

Stanley, J. C. 1957a. "Index of Means vs. Means of Indices." American Journal of Psychology 70: 467-68.

____. 1957b. "KR-20 as the Stepped-up Mean Item Intercorrelation." Fourteenth Yearbook of the National Council on Measurement in Education, pp. 78-92. Ames, Iowa: National Council on Measurement in Education.

Sundberg, N. D., and Tyler, L. E. 1962. Clinical Psychology. New York: Appleton-Century-Crofts.

Terman, L. M. 1916. The Measurement of Intelligence. Boston: Houghton Mifflin.

____. 1919. The Intelligence of School Children. Boston: Houghton Mifflin.

Thorndike, R. L., ed. 1971. Educational Measurement. 2nd ed. Washington, D.C.: American Council on Education.

Thurstone, L. L. 1938. Primary Mental Abilities. Psychometric Monographs, No. 1. Chicago: University of Chicago Press.

_____, and Thurstone, T. G. 1941. "Factorial Studies of Intelligence." Psychometric Monographs 2.

Tinsley, B. E. A. 1971. "An Investigation of the Rasch Simple Logistic Model for Tests of Intelligence or Attainment." Ph.D. diss. University of Minnesota.

Wherry, R. J., and Gaylord, R. H. 1944. "Factor Pattern of Test Items and Tests as a Function of the Correlation Coefficient, Content, Difficulty, and Constant Error Factors." Psychometrika 144: 237-44.

Whitely, S. E., and Dawis, R. V. 1974. "The Nature of Objectivity with the Rasch Model." Journal of Educational Measurement, Fall 11: 163-78.

_____, and _____. 1976. "The Influence of Test Context on Item Difficulty." Educational and Psychological Measurement 36: 329-37.

Willmott, A. S., and Fowles, D. E. 1974. The Objective Interpretation of Test Performance. England: National Foundation for Educational Research.

Winer, B. J. 1971. Statistical Principles in Experimental Design. 2nd ed. New York: McGraw-Hill.

Woodcock, R. W., and Dahl, M. N. 1976. A Common Scale for the Measurement of Person Ability and Test Item Difficulty. Circle Pines, Minn.: American Guidance Service.

Worthing, A. G., and Giffner, J. 1943. Treatment of Experimental Data. New York: Wiley, pp. 252-55.

Wright, B. D. 1967. "Sample-free Test Calibration and Person Measurement." Paper presented at Invitational Conference on Testing Problems, Educational Testing Service, Princeton, New Jersey, October 18.

_____. 1975. Sample-free Test Calibration and Person Measurement. A.E.R.A. presession, 1975.

____, and Douglas, Graham A. 1974. "Best Test Design." Manuscript. Chicago: University of Chicago.

____, and Mead, R. J. 1975. "CALFIT Sample-Free Item Calibration with a Rasch Measurement Model." Chicago: University of Chicago Research Memorandum 18, March.

____, and Panchapakesan, N. 1969. "A Procedure for Sample-Free Item Analysis." Educational and Psychological Measurement, Spring 29: 23-48.

Yerkes, R. M., ed. 1921. "Psychological Examining in the U.S. Army." Memoirs of the National Academy of Sciences 15.

ABOUT THE AUTHOR

ROBERT M. HASHWAY received his Ph. D. in educational research, measurement, and evaluation from Boston College in 1977. Under the direction of Dr. George F. Madaus, Dr. Hashway completed his dissertation comparing Rasch and traditionally constructed tests. While working at Boston College, Dr. Hashway served as principal investigator of a longitudinal study involving police officers funded by the Law Enforcement Assistance Administration. He has served as senior research associate on various projects involving vocational education and coping behavior during disasters. Dr. Hashway also holds a Master's degree in mathematics from Rhode Island College. He has published numerous articles in the American Mathematics Monthly, Mathematics Magazine, and the American Journal of Physics. He has also published in Educational and Psychological Measurement and the Educational Research Quarterly.

RELATED TITLES
Published by
Praeger Special Studies

PERSPECTIVES ON IMPROVING EDUCATION:
Project TALENT's Young Adults Look Back

edited by John C. Flanagan

STUDENT ATTITUDES AND ACADEMIC ENVIRONMENTS:
A Study of California Higher Education

Harvey E. Rich
Pamela M. Jolicoeur